Stories of Past Lives, Dreams, and Soul Travel

Also by Harold Klemp

Past Lives, Dreams, and Soul Travel

Animals Are Soul Too!

The Art of Spiritual Dreaming

Ask the Master, Books 1 and 2

Autobiography of a Modern Prophet

Child in the Wilderness

A Cosmic Sea of Words: The ECKANKAR Lexicon

ECK Masters and You: An Illustrated Guide

Is Life a Random Walk?

The Living Word, Books 1 and 2

A Modern Prophet Answers Your Key Questions about Life

Soul Travelers of the Far Country

The Spiritual Exercises of ECK

The Spiritual Laws of Life

The Temple of ECK

Those Wonderful ECK Masters

The Wind of Change

Wisdom of the Heart, Books 1 and 2

Your Road Map to the ECK Teachings: ECKANKAR Study Guide

Youth Ask a Modern Prophet about Life, Love, and God

The Mahanta Transcripts Series

Journey of Soul, Book 1

How to Find God, Book 2

The Secret Teachings, Book 3

The Golden Heart, Book 4

Cloak of Consciousness, Book 5

Unlocking the Puzzle Box, Book 6

The Eternal Dreamer, Book 7

The Dream Master, Book 8

We Come as Eagles, Book 9

The Drumbeat of Time, Book 10

What Is Spiritual Freedom? Book 11

How the Inner Master Works, Book 12

The Slow Burning Love of God, Book 13

The Secret of Love, Book 14

Our Spiritual Wake-Up Calls, Book 15

How to Survive Spiritually in Our Times, Book 16

The Immortality of Soul Series

The Language of Soul

Love—The Keystone of Life

Touching the Face of God

Truth Has No Secrets

Spiritual Wisdom Series

Spiritual Wisdom on Conquering Fear

Spiritual Wisdom on Health and Healing

Stories to Help You See God in Your Life

The Book of ECK Parables, Volume 1

The Book of ECK Parables, Volume 2

The Book of ECK Parables, Volume 3

Stories to Help You See God in Your Life, ECK Parables, Book 4

MAHANTA

This book has been edited by and published under the supervision of the Mahanta, the Living ECK Master, Sri Harold Klemp.

Stories of Past Lives, Dreams, and Soul Travel

Harold Klemp, Series Editor

ECKANKAR
Minneapolis

Stories of Past Lives, Dreams, and Soul Travel

The terms ECKANKAR, ECK, EK, MAHANTA, SOUL TRAVEL, and VAIRAGI, among others, are trademarks of ECKANKAR, PO Box 2000, Chanhassen, MN 55317-2000 USA.   020403

Printed in USA
Compiled by John Kulick
Edited by Joan Klemp, Anthony Moore,
and Mary Carroll Moore

Library of Congress Cataloging-in-Publication Data

Stories of past lives, dreams, and soul travel / [edited by] Harold Klemp.
     p. cm.
   ISBN 1-57043-191-4 (alk. paper)
     1. Eckankar (Organization)—Doctrines.   2. Reincarnation—Eckankar (Organization) 3. Dreams—Religious aspects—Eckankar (Organization) 4. Astral projection. I. Klemp, Harold.

BP605.E3.S76 2004
299'.93 — dc21

                                        2003049026

∞ This paper meets the requirements of ANSI/NISO Z39.48-1992 (Permanence of Paper).

Contents

Part Three: Soul Travel

Foreword

The teachings of ECK define the nature of Soul. You are Soul, a particle of God sent into this world to gain spiritual experience.

The goal in ECK is spiritual freedom in this lifetime, after which you become a Co-worker with God, both here and in the next world. Karma and reincarnation are primary beliefs.

Key to the ECK teachings is the Mahanta, the Living ECK Master. He has the special ability to act as both the Inner and Outer Master for ECK students. The prophet of Eckankar, he is given respect but is not worshiped. He teaches the sacred name of God, HU. When sung just a few minutes each day, HU will lift you spiritually into the Light and Sound of God—the ECK (Holy Spirit). This easy spiritual exercise and others will purify you. You are then able to accept the full love of God in this lifetime.

Sri Harold Klemp is the Mahanta, the Living ECK Master today. Author of many books, discourses, and articles, he teaches the ins and outs of the spiritual life. His teachings lift people and help them recognize and understand their own experiences in the Light and Sound of God. Audio and video recordings of many of his talks are available to you.

Stories of Past Lives, Dreams, and Soul Travel will

show you, through experiences of people just like you, how very much God loves you.

To find out more about Harold Klemp and Eckankar, please turn to pages 275–79 in the back of this book.

Introduction

The stories that follow are accounts of God's people doing godly things.

Past lives, dreams, and Soul Travel are of great importance to the spiritual life. A true knowledge and practice of them leads to the most satisfying and fulfilling life you could ever imagine—or wish for.

And here it is, the inspiration to help you on your own journey to God.

How does the Holy Spirit, the ECK, relate to us? Read these stories and learn of many ways in which God talks to people. What does God say? Are the divine messages of universal reach, or are they love whisperings for us alone?

And why does God speak?

Read the stories in this book, and you'll find many answers to questions of your own. The stories come from every walk of life. They were chosen with you in mind.

Today is a special time in the history of mankind. It is now possible to tell of past lives, dreams, and Soul Travel without fear of censure, persecution, or worse. A window of opportunity is open. It has opened for you.

What makes a spiritual life? Read and see. Do you want freedom, knowledge, truth, or wisdom? Love?

Look no further. The passkey is in your hands. Feel free to use it.

Here is the key to your spiritual heritage. Learn who and what you are through the stories of these travelers on the path of ECK. They are like you. They love God, life, and its many blessings.

Oh, read and you'll see. You'll understand. Of that I am sure. So come. We can talk on the way.

Harold Klemp

Part One

Past Lives

A past-life recall told him of another lifetime when he was a young woman among the Mayans.

1

Getting Answers from God through Past Lives, Dreams, and Soul Travel

Harold Klemp

Most all his life, a certain man harbored a stubborn fear of life. This fear robbed him of happiness and vitality, often leaving him angry and full of self-pity. He couldn't understand it or break its hold.

Years later, he became a member of Eckankar. His outlook on living improved in many ways after that time, but this fear of life remained at the borders of his consciousness, always ready to pour water upon the fires of his hopes and dreams. Then one day, he finally learned the reason for that haunting fear.

Past Lives

An Eckankar seminar near his home featured a HU Chant on Sunday morning before the regular program.

A HU Chant is a spiritual exercise. For a half hour or so, a group of people sing HU, an ancient name for God. It is a strikingly beautiful song, much like a Gregorian chant sung by a large group of singers.

Early that Sunday morning, about three or four

o'clock, he had a dim memory of a dream about the ancient Mayans and a past life he had spent as one. But he fell asleep again and forgot the details.

At seven-thirty he arose, dressed, and traveled about forty minutes to the seminar. He put his attention upon "the Mayan thing" during the HU Chant.

His Spiritual Eye opened.

A past-life recall told him of another lifetime when he was a young woman among the Mayans. In that life, she was very beautiful. The beauty came of her intense love for life, which brought happiness and joy to everyone who knew her. Her very atoms breathed this exultation.

Unfortunately, her beauty also caught the attention of the temple priest, who always kept an eye out for human sacrifice worthy of the Mayan god whose stone image sat with cupped hands before the temple. The priest cut out her heart while it was still beating.

This man, looking back on that lifetime as a beautiful woman, now knew the reason for his fear of life.

Never since had he been able to recapture such a love of life. But he also realized the reason he had come to Eckankar—a chance to restore that love to his life. Yet the old fear always lurked in the shadows. All his life, he had the instinctive feeling a fatal blow would strike him if he ever again loved too much.

Singing HU had opened his heart to God.

In some way, God's love will open our hearts so that we have the courage to face the darkest secrets from our past.

God speaks to us through past lives, dreams, and Soul Travel. The above example illustrates how Divine Spirit, the Voice of God, told one man the reason for his longstanding fear of life.

Dreams

The play of karma underlies all human relationships.

In this next story, a young man gets to balance the scales of justice from the past. He needed to repay a victim from a previous life, but the Mahanta, the Living ECK Master (the spiritual leader of Eckankar today) sent a dream to prepare him for the necessary, though painful experience.

Nick, a name we'll use to insure his privacy, had a dream in which a beautiful young woman came to the office. She was trying to use the phone on his manager's desk. Nick and the girl felt an immediate attraction for each other in the dream, and soon they began a passionate romance. But, to his frustration, it led nowhere.

Then he awoke.

Some weeks later, a young student came to the office to get work experience. Nick loved her from the start. He did everything in his power to win her heart, but she coyly brushed aside his passion with promises. Later, always later. Soon everyone in the office was talking about their relationship.

Then the sky fell in.

Through the office grapevine, Nick learned that this young woman had been having a secret love affair with his best friend at work. It had begun nearly the first week that she had arrived there. Worse, Nick had set the stage. One night that first week he had to work late, so he asked his good friend to take her home. That was the beginning of the end.

Only the ECK, Divine Spirit, kept Nick from losing his mind when he learned of the secret love affair. But he turned sour on life. Why had this beautiful young woman come—to purposely bring him grief?

In his anxiety and anger, he even forgot about the spiritual love of the Mahanta, the Living ECK Master.

Then came a second dream. As the Inner Master, the Mahanta took him on the Time Track and showed him a past life in which he had been a woman. Married to a wealthy man, this individual had two house servants, both of whom suffered due to Nick's misuse of position and authority. One was this student.

"You made that karma," the Mahanta explained. "That debt stands between you and God's love. Pay now and be done with it."

In the end, Nick recognized the hand of karma and the long, outstanding debt that he needed to settle. It took awhile for the crushing pain to subside, of course, but now he's happy he settled the debt. After the pain had finally gone, Nick felt a new sense of freedom and lightness. God's love could now shine more directly into his heart. That obstructing block of karmic debt was gone.

Dreams are thus a second way that we get answers from God.

Soul Travel

What is Soul Travel?

Soul Travel is a more direct, conscious way to transcend the human consciousness in order to hear God speak through Its voice, the Holy Spirit. Most saints in history knew this ancient science of Soul Travel. They used it often during their prayers or meditations.

A very new member of Eckankar, Melissa (a pseudonym) did the Spiritual Exercises of ECK every day during her first two months of studying the ECK discourses. These are monthly lessons in the spiritual works that the Mahanta, the Living ECK Master usually sends to ECKists for the expansion of consciousness.

Most discourses have a special exercise each month.

Melissa went into contemplation before going to bed. The Light of God filled her Spiritual Eye, and a few notes of music (the Sound of God) followed.

Then came the sound of rushing air or wind. She was moving in her true spiritual form, the Soul body. But suddenly doubt and fear filled her heart. A former Pentecostal, she immediately called out the name of Jesus. Things started to go in reverse. Where once she had moved forward, she was now traveling backward in the spiritual worlds.

Quickly, she caught herself.

Melissa told herself that she would put her complete faith and trust in the Mahanta. Again she moved forward. The lesson gained from this Soul Travel experience was that if she placed her trust in anyone other than the Mahanta, she would indeed regress instead of moving forward spiritually.

That is an example of Soul Travel. It was God's way of telling Melissa that it was time for her to move on to the high spiritual teachings of ECK. She had graduated from the primary schools of religion. Now it was time to return home to God.

Past lives, dreams, and Soul Travel are all part of Eckankar. They can help open your spiritual ears to the divine love that surrounds you every minute of every day.

Look into the ECK teachings. You will find they are charged with the energy of life and love. Those qualities can be yours too.

Today.

2

A Past-Life Dream Shows the Future

Julie Olson

I met my husband in 1986 while living in New York City. Oddly enough, my parents immediately began pressuring me to marry him.

This was totally out of character with their usual "hands-off" approach to my life. I was an independent and sometimes rebellious daughter who had proven I could run my own life. But I was strangely acquiescent to their suggestions. I allowed my mother to choose the church, pick the most convenient weekend for the wedding, and rule in favor of a tiny ceremony.

In fact, only my parents, my fiancé, and a close friend were present. My four siblings and other close friends were strangely excluded.

I had asked the Inner Master before the wedding if I was doing the right thing. The image I got was simply a green traffic light. So I trusted my guidance and went ahead with the plans.

When we arrived at the small church in Brooklyn, the priest ushered us into a small office. He had never met us, but he obviously felt a need to fulfill his ecclesiastical duties. He spent the next forty-five minutes explaining the many pitfalls of marriage, especially with the added pressures of living in New York City.

The ceremony finally took place, and we left for dinner at a favorite restaurant.

Two months later my youngest brother came to visit. We took him for a walk after dinner to show him the small, old church where we married. A few blocks from the church I saw the priest who'd married us.

I walked up and cheerfully said, "Hello!" The priest, who was dressed in street clothes, drew a blank.

"Don't you remember us?" I asked, sweeping my arm toward my husband. The priest said, "No, should I?"

I blurted, "You married us about two months ago." Now he was embarrassed and tried a joking tone, saying, "You must have been dressed differently."

We laughed nervously together and left. My face was burning, and my mind spinning. How could he not remember us after that long lecture? It was a disturbing waking dream, whose symbolism I had not begun to grasp. But in time I would.

Over the course of the next few months, my new husband became extremely possessive. He even began to accuse me of having an affair. I became afraid to go out with friends for fear of accusations. Even though I was doing my spiritual exercises every night and trusting the Mahanta, I felt a prisoner in the marriage. I knew there had to be a lesson. I finally asked the Mahanta to show me why I was in this situation.

About three nights later I had a profound dream.

I was flying above a white clapboard farmstead. There was a crude fence around the yard. As I flew closer, the image froze like a still picture and then released so I could approach. This happened several times until I found myself in the body of a black woman, around thirty years old, who was sitting on the grass, crying.

I immediately knew who she was and had access
to all her memories, feelings, and experiences. I was
married with two young sons, age eight and ten (my
husband and children were in the yard). I was known
for my ability to sing beautifully. And I was very, very
unhappy.

Then more unfolded as I observed and participated
in several memories of that lifetime.

I went back in time until I was about eighteen,
living in a small rural area farmed by a community of
black families. It was the late 1800s. My father was
reasonably successful and known in the community as
a strong and religious man.

At this time, I was meeting a young man by a river
almost every day. He worked on a nearby farm. We
would sit for hours watching the river and talking.

We never kissed or even held hands, but I was
desperately in love with this handsome young man. I
knew he felt the same about me. My days revolved
around the time I spent talking with him. It seemed
he could see right through to my innermost self. But
one day, before we even got to express our true feelings,
my father announced I was to marry the son of a friend
of his, also a successful farmer. I protested, thinking
of the young man whom I met by the river. But my
father would hear none of it.

In the next scene I was in a country church plead-
ing with the minister, telling him I could not marry this
man. He was not the one I loved! The minister turned
a deaf ear to my cries.

I knew the young man by the river had heard of
my marriage. Thinking I did not love him after all, he
left town brokenhearted. My pain and sorrow increased
with each year of my loveless marriage, as I poured all
my heart and love into a memory. I stopped singing and

neglected my husband and sons.

The dream rolled forward until I found myself back in the body of the adult woman at the start of the dream. It was about twelve years after the wedding. I was crying because a man had come to the back door that morning. He had a dirty blanket over his head and was asking for food. He was obviously a vagrant, and having just baked some biscuits, I put them in an old cloth and passed them to him. Something in his eyes brought me up short. Embarrassed by his bold, intense look, I went back into the house.

Later, I had the most painful realization that the vagrant was my true love from years before. He had come not to get food, but to see how I was faring. His look of intense love had startled me. Then the dream ended.

I awoke the next morning and wrote the dream down. I had spent that lifetime in somewhat useless pain and grief. The love I had in my heart was locked up for only one unavailable person. As a result my husband and sons had received very little from me.

How did this relate to my present situation? Did I need to give more love to my husband in this life? Maybe he was the arranged-marriage husband from that time.

But who was the man I truly loved? It would be a while until the ECK showed me the full scope of the dream.

Meanwhile, my husband's jealousy and temper raged out of control. It was like living with a complete stranger. About this time, I also became very ill and was hospitalized with a severe blood infection. I had a 40 percent chance of survival. I had no will to live under the conditions of my marriage as they were. But during my hospitalization I had a near-death experience that put my life into precise and sharp perspective. I lost my fear of death—and ironically, my fear of living.

Trusting the ECK, I took control of my life. It took a few months, but I finally moved out and sought a divorce, which was finalized just ten short months after the wedding. The karma we shared seemed to evaporate once I made the decision to leave.

Odd things happened: We were let out of our apartment lease, our bank account dissolved (due to a bank error), and I found a new job which took me into a new set of daily circumstances. The ECK swiftly carried me into a new life.

All this time, I remembered the dream and was determined to discover why I'd entered such a destructive relationship. I saw that a disturbing pattern had developed. Why had I never seemed to find the kind, gentle love I longed for?

Apparently some part of me felt I deserved a bond that was not kind but possessive, jealous, even destructive. But Divine Spirit was giving me a chance to break this pattern.

First, I had to give *myself* the kind of deep love I imagined. I sang HU every night and developed more trust in my guide, the Mahanta. I learned to love myself as Soul, a divine spark of God, and I slowly began to heal.

Nine months later, I attended the 1987 ECK Worldwide Seminar in Houston. I was waiting with friends for a table at a restaurant when another group of seminar attendees arrived. We didn't know them, but we invited them to sit at our table.

I felt an electric shock go through me when I first saw one of the men. Though I'd never laid eyes on him before, I wanted to shout, "What are *you* doing here!"

I was filled with an odd mixture of joy, laughter, and incredulity. The feeling passed as we sat down to dinner, but during the next few days at the seminar, this man and I kept bumping into each other.

One evening after sitting and talking in the hotel lobby, we exchanged addresses. I promised to keep in touch with him, but I had no interest in anything other than a friendship. Over the course of the next year, we met at Eckankar seminars, spoke on the phone, and wrote letters. We spent hours talking—I could tell him anything. I remember thinking what a dear friend he had become.

One year after meeting him, during the 1988 ECK Worldwide Seminar, it finally hit me: I had a deep love for this man. I moved to Iowa where he lived, and Paul and I were married.

I had forgotten about the past-life dream until one day when Paul and I were talking about his recurring neck problem. He had gone to several chiropractors, but it wasn't until he had a dream about a past life that the source of the problem was revealed.

In his dream he had been a black man, a vagrant in the late 1800s. He died when a group of white men found him sleeping in a shack and hung him.

I felt my own past-life dream come back into my consciousness with a zing! Paul was my love from that previous life! The long talks by the river mirrored our long talks in this life.

I also realized my mother in this lifetime had been my father then, forcing my marriage in both incarnations. My husband in that difficult lifetime had indeed been my jealous first husband in this one. Ten months in an emotional prison was the price I had to pay for a life where he received no love from me. My two sons from that lifetime are now my two younger brothers.

They had arrived in our family while I was a teenager, and I was able to help raise them and nurture them in this lifetime—as I hadn't in that one. I have a very deep love for them, and they've always felt like my own children.

The priest who couldn't remember my marriage in New York City, despite having performed it himself after giving us a forty-five-minute lecture, seemed to mirror the minister who had married me in my past life. That minister had turned a blind eye and deaf ear to my pleas of not wanting to marry.

Despite the difficulty of the first marriage, I am grateful for it now because it brought me to a greater understanding of myself. I now know that all experiences point to one great spiritual lesson: how to give divine love first to yourself and then others. And this has led me to a greater love of God.

It also brought me together again with the man by the river!

3

The Gift of Awareness

Karen Candito

When I was fourteen years old, my father arranged a family outing. My sister and I spent one Saturday cruising with him on a naval aircraft carrier. There were hundreds of other civilians like us on board, but the ship was so massive that no one felt crowded.

For a large portion of the day I wandered around the ship alone. I felt confident and wonderfully free. Being an awkward teenage girl, it surprised me to find that the order and precision (which is so much a part of military life) gave me a familiar sense of stability and security.

That entire day, I also felt unusually connected to my father, as if we were two sailors sharing a sacred moment. I wanted to stay forever.

Twenty years later, at the age of thirty-four, I found myself facing problems in my family life. I noticed myself getting unreasonably impatient with my children, who were eight and ten years old at the time, for small things like not cleaning their rooms in the exact way I'd insisted upon or not setting the table exactly right. If my husband didn't put the newspaper away where it belonged just after reading it, I became irritated and let him know it.

It suddenly became obvious that life didn't flow for me unless my family followed my demanding and inflexible rules.

What was this rigidity that I was trying to impose on my family? How much longer could they live with my need to control everything they did? Why did I have such an inner need to discipline life in every tiny detail? I knew I had to release myself from something, but I was afraid to face what that something was.

Whenever I encounter a spiritual stumbling block like this, I like to do one of the Spiritual Exercises of ECK. I sit quietly, close my eyes, and sing HU, an ancient name for God. This particular evening I asked Wah Z (the spiritual name of Sri Harold Klemp, the Mahanta, the Living ECK Master) for help and insight into my problem. Shortly after, I had a dream.

In the dream I was back on the deck of an aircraft carrier, with the brisk sea air caressing my face. I felt the same peace and contentment I had felt that wonderful day on the ship when I was fourteen.

Then I looked down at myself and discovered that I was a man. A Japanese man standing on the deck of a Japanese ship! I realized that in a previous lifetime, I had been a sailor in the Japanese navy.

I had the memory of loving that life. I loved the freedom, the travel, and my distinguished military career. In that lifetime, I felt successful and was content with myself. The love I experienced in that life explained why I had felt so strong, free, and connected on the aircraft carrier in this lifetime.

I also saw in the dream that I had carried some habits and attitudes from that incarnation into this one—characteristics that were not helpful now.

I was trying to impose the rules and regulations, which had made my past military life comfortable, on my present family. How could I expect my loved ones to live life on a military schedule or to make beds so tight a dime could bounce off them?

Somehow I had connected my memories of freedom and contentment with regimentation and discipline. I had been afraid to trust that I could be free and content without my inflexible rules.

We so often hold on to past-life habits and ideas no longer useful to us in our present state of consciousness. With the help of the Mahanta, I am learning to work with the rhythm of life. I am learning that letting go of old, worn-out ideas doesn't mean losing other things, like security or happiness. I have everything I need right here and now.

4

Dissolving Karma
with Others the Easy Way

Giovanni Riva

always thought I had a good relationship with my mother. But I had never been able to openly express my love for her. Like many men, I would give her love indirectly and hope she knew. But as I grew spiritually, I wanted to learn more about this reluctance to give love openly to others. I began to look at other people's behavior with loved ones.

One day I realized that my mother was also rather undemonstrative. As Soul I saw how I had chosen my family in this life. My mother's coolness was nothing more than my own beliefs and behavior—maybe from past lives—coming back to me.

One way my mother did show her love was through food. In my profession as a TV cameraman, I often work through mealtimes, and sometimes I stop by my mother's house on the way home.

Even if she is in the middle of doing something else, she immediately asks me if I have eaten. If I haven't, she jumps up and starts cooking. And as I sit at the table to eat, she sits with me to keep me company.

A long time passed before I realized how much love these small events contained. Still, in my daily spiritual exercises, I asked the Mahanta, my spiritual guide, to teach me how to love my mother in a more open, sincere way.

Soon an opportunity arose.

One day my mother called and asked me to take her from Switzerland to Italy to open up her other house for a visit. At that moment I perceived a gift. I agreed to accompany her.

The morning of our trip, I got up and did a spiritual exercise and asked my guide, the Mahanta, to help me make this day truly special for my mother. I was determined to start a new cycle. Love was the goal, and I would make myself totally available for anything she needed.

En route, we talked. I listened to everything she had to say, we laughed, and we also shared some moments of silence. At one point I felt the need to hold her hand, something we had never done. I knew this was my golden opportunity to begin a new relationship with her. So with courage I took her hand gently in mine. My mother looked at me with surprise but then smiled and accepted my gesture. I felt love flowing freely between us.

As we neared our destination, I invited my mother to lunch, telling her she should order whatever she wanted. We had a wonderful time and shared much laughter.

I could tell a great healing was on the way.

When we got to the house, I opened all the doors and windows and turned on the electricity and water. I went to ask my mother what my next chore was and found her outside cutting wood. I told her I would cut the wood so she could work inside. Hours later when I was cutting the last big logs, she came back and offered to help me.

As we were sawing the logs, I felt something change.

We were having a lot of fun, and when our gaze met there was a new sense of joy and love never before experienced.

The last log proved extremely difficult to cut. With a big smile, my mother said aloud, "Oh, there must be a knot."

Instantly, I understood this was a bit of Golden-tongued Wisdom in which Divine Spirit was telling me some piece of inner truth. I thanked the Mahanta and said to myself: *Now I understand.* There was a knot of unresolved karma (effects from the past) between us that kept my mother and me from unconditional love. The Mahanta was helping me cut through this knot of past experiences. And my mother was helping me dissolve the old attitude with generous and joyous laughter!

I realized that old behavior patterns can be completely erased with the help of the Inner Master. This subtle experience helped me to open my heart and love others in a new way.

5

Repaying a Debt from Viking Days

Joan Bryden

*S*everal years ago I attended an Eckankar meeting in Bendigo, Victoria, Australia. In the public hall where the meeting was held, my attention was drawn to a line drawing of a Viking ship pinned to a notice board.

Instantly, I felt as though cold water had been poured down my back. Over the years, I have associated this sensation with the sudden revelation of truth. I knew the Mahanta, my inner guide, was telling me: "You lived a previous life as a Viking, and it has some bearing on your life right now." However, I soon forgot about this insight, or waking dream.

Several weeks later, in conversation with other members of Eckankar, my experience came back to me and I mentioned it. Two of them said they also remembered being Vikings. One recalled a vicious battle on a beach, where she received a fatal blow to the chest from a battle-ax.

About this time I took a position as a companion and housekeeper for an elderly lady. She constantly complained of having a sore neck. I would sympathize, saying I quite understood since mine often felt bad also.

One day, while I was absently doing the ironing, the Mahanta presented me with a vision. Vivid pictures flashed before my mind's eye: I am in a battle on a beach in Britain. I'm a Viking, swinging a battle-ax. An enemy soldier is standing with his back to me. I swing the ax down into the junction of his neck and shoulder. He collapses and dies. Almost immediately, somebody does the same thing to me. Exit that life.

Whew! That was intense. I thought. But what did it mean?

It was not until some days later, when my mind was once again lulled by the monotony of chores, that the Viking scene appeared again. This time another realization dawned on me: my current employer was the soldier I had killed in that battle long ago!

It certainly explains why we both have bad necks, I thought wryly. I began to ask the Mahanta if payment was due for that blow so long ago. By how much had I shortened her life when I killed her in that battle?

As the months went on, I thought about this each time I massaged my employer's neck and shoulders. The feeling of rightness was so strong I would think, *This time I am making her life better instead of wrecking it.*

I had worked for her for seven and a half months when the woman died very suddenly of a heart attack. I was comforted in that she did not suffer. And as I contemplated the situation in my daily ECK spiritual exercises, I knew in my heart that I had repaid my debt. I had just worked out an important piece of karma. Now I was ready to move on.

Messages from the Mahanta had clued me in to the past life and helped me make the most of my opportunity to return love and heal an old wound. My neck feels better too.

6

I Am Always with You

John Hammontree

I began having nightmares. I was always underground, underwater, or in a confined space where I couldn't breathe. I would wake up terrified, sure I was dying of suffocation.

I asked the Mahanta, my inner teacher, to show me the past-life source of these nightmares.

Several nights later, I awakened at 1:15 a.m. from a deep sleep. Following a strong nudge, I went to sit in my chair in the living room, looking forward to a Soul Travel experience or the past-life memory I had requested.

It began like a dream or a movie in my head. I could see my family and me being rousted from our home into a freezing cold night by Russian soldiers. I saw a wall of white eight to ten feet high, which looked like snow. The soldiers were standing in front of it, training their rifles on us. On command they began to shoot.

Although I was hit and couldn't move, I was still alive. We were thrown onto a cart and hauled to a place where we were thrown into a ditch. Then the soldiers began covering us with shovelfuls of dirt, snow, and rocks.

"I'm alive. Don't cover me or I'll die," I screamed inwardly. But of course they couldn't hear me. They kept filling the hole. In that life I died a frightening death of suffocation.

When I awoke from my contemplation, I was sure I had seen the last of my nightmares for now I understood their source.

The next day an out-of-town friend called. I told her about my past-life memory of the night before. When I mentioned the Russian soldiers, she finished for me:

"They dragged us out, shot us, and then threw us on a cart, took us out, and buried us. I was there, John. I was there!" We marveled over our shared experience.

Well, that night I had the granddaddy of all nightmares. I was too overwhelmed by my fear to even ask the Mahanta for help. I had thought that simply viewing the past life would be enough to release me from my fear. But clearly I still had work to do.

Sometime later, I was talking to another friend about my nightmares. "Why don't you ask the Mahanta to take you by the hand and walk you through the fear?" he asked.

It made sense.

Why hadn't I thought of that? In my daily spiritual exercises, I began to ask the Mahanta to please help me through the fear, as I couldn't do it by myself. After that I had a few more nightmares, but each time the Mahanta was with me, reassuring me.

I no longer wake in terror each night. And I know the truth of the ancient promise of the Mahanta, the Living ECK Master: I am always with you.

I found myself observing a past life. The detail was rich beyond compare, and I knew the three people I saw were myself, my husband, and Tom.

7

Awakening to the Past

Carol Hidle

*S*ometimes insights flow through me just after I wake up in the morning. Often I glimpse things more clearly or receive answers to problems I've turned over to the Mahanta before sleep.

One of the biggest ongoing problems is my relationship with my stepson. Tom moved from his mother's house to ours when he was eleven. He and my husband are close, but Tom and I have an undercurrent of antipathy. This has been a source of great sadness to me, for it has been very difficult to show the same love for Tom that I have for my other stepson and son. The trouble is seldom overt. We try to keep harmony, to honor our family.

Over the years, I've asked the Mahanta, Wah Z (Sri Harold Klemp's spiritual name), for understanding. Finally, one morning I had a breakthrough. I found myself observing a past life. The detail was rich beyond compare, and I knew the three people I saw were myself, my husband, and Tom.

It was the late 1800s in a Swiss-Tyrolean setting, where the men wore lederhosen. My husband was married to a woman then who is Tom in this incarnation. He cared for her very much and didn't want to hurt her, but he also loved me, a younger woman.

We lived in a small village, and our love affair was common knowledge. I was fascinated to see what we all looked like in that life—the vivid detail of the clothes, the sounds, and the smells of that time. My vision even caught the unironed wrinkles in the blouses and shirts, and the roughness of the cloth.

As I observed all this, I found myself feeling sympathy for Tom, the wife. I could understand my rivalry with this Soul, which gave me a much broader view of our relationship.

I realized that past life was the basis for the friction between us. And I suddenly understood why my husband was especially considerate of Tom's feelings. As the days passed, I didn't feel as resentful when he was occasionally lenient with Tom.

This past-life recall brought more love and understanding into our family. I am better able to take control of my thoughts and actions.

I would love to say that Tom and I now see eye-to-eye. The karma from the past is mostly still here, but my heart and viewpoint have changed. When I observe similar problems in other families, I sympathize. The Mahanta has truly given me a gift that has made my life richer, smoother, and more loving.

8

I Knew My Wife
in a Past Life

Daniel Tardent

*M*y partner, Josse, and I have always enjoyed a very special relationship. When
we met, there was an instant feeling of
recognition which has stayed with us. We enjoy a great
sense of love and spiritual togetherness in our marriage.

However, about a year ago I erupted from my usual
calm state into a series of explosions. I felt angry most
of the time and struggled for control.

Like a volcano, I would fume for hours, until finally
I could control it no longer. The worst part was Josse
was the focal point of my anger. Everything she did
annoyed me—for no reason. I would get so wild I wanted
to pick up the nearest fragile thing and throw it.
Sometimes I did just that.

As an ECKist I know anger is one of the five passions
of the mind. We learn self-discipline through the spiritual exercises. Finding a larger perspective had always
been easy for me before. In fact, I'd never really had
to deal with anger much before.

I felt confused and upset—me, a previously calm
and well-balanced person, suddenly out of control. I
felt like two people: one who was slowly losing his
mind, and the other who was calmly observing the

destructive effects of anger on me and my loved ones.

I continued my spiritual exercises. I asked my inner guide, the Mahanta, for help. At first things just seemed to get worse.

Pretty soon, I stopped feeling anything. I had closed down. That evening, when I no longer cared, the Mahanta gave me two dreams.

The first notes in my dream journal for that night: "I've gone absolutely wild. Breaking things, screaming. Josse is around. I'm in a total rage." Later in the night I dreamed again: "I lie on the ground, badly wounded. Around me a swirling vortex of men and horses scramble for their lives. The red dust blows hot on my face as I slip into shock. The air is violent. I am a Sioux warrior in a fierce tribal battle."

I've had vivid past-life recollections before, but the experience always resembled watching a movie on a screen. This time was different. I was caught in the movie! Nothing could have prepared me for the horror, pain, and fear I experienced in this dream: "A large white horse wheeled around me. My heart opened as I saw my tribal chief watching over me. I knew I was safe now, and I struggled to call out. But as his horse reared, the chief thrust his spear—with all his strength—into the place where my neck and shoulder met.

"The shock and pain of the impact were immense. I stared desperately at him as my world melted into hot blackness. In that moment his face changed and I was looking at Josse astride the big white horse.

"I left my body quickly and rage overcame me. The chief who I had loved and trusted with my life had betrayed and killed me!"

I woke up from the dream in a cold sweat. I could still feel the force of the impact of the spear in my neck.

I wondered if I would ever be able to forgive Josse for betraying me in that lifetime.

My understanding of past-life healing had been very simplistic. Once you saw the cause of a situation, it would disappear, replaced with a great feeling of love and understanding. But I was full of sickness and anger. I told Josse about the Sioux dream, feeling my rage stir again.

As we talked, however, the light of Divine Spirit began to glow. With it came a deeper insight into the truth of my dream: I had been very badly wounded in battle. Because of the intense fighting, there was no possibility of saving me. The terrible tortures I would suffer as a captive of the enemy tribe were well known. So my chief had done the most loving thing: he had killed me quickly and released me to freedom in the inner worlds.

Finally, I understood. The insight poured balm on an old, old wound.

As the weeks passed, my new understanding of what had happened in that lifetime slowly filtered into all levels of my being. I became less intense in my outlook on life. It was as though a heavy gray cloud had been lifted from me.

The wild mood swings vanished. I could trust life again. For the first time in many months I was happy.

The most wonderful gift was the new love I felt for Josse. Our bond of love as Sioux warriors filled me with awe. It was the love of two Souls committed to helping each other on the journey home to God—a love which continues to grow.

I learned many things through this experience. But the lesson that really stays with me is simply this: The Spiritual Exercises of ECK and the inner guide, the Mahanta, can help solve any problem.

9

Love Lost—Love Found

Debbie Johnson

hy couldn't I find true and lasting love? The answer to that question was beyond me. The men I dated seemed nice enough, but every time I found one I liked he left me and married one of my friends. This went on for about fifteen years.

I wondered what qualities make a woman lovable. I didn't have a clue.

I read self-help books and tried therapy, getting in better shape, and dressing in a more feminine way. And, of course, I tried begging the Inner Master. Over and over I asked for help in my spiritual exercises. I needed love so much. I felt devastated by the idea of living life alone.

Finally, I looked within myself for the answer. Eckankar had taught me that actions from our past lives don't just evaporate. We continue to weave the threads from past lifetimes into this one.

I began to wonder if I had been a womanizer in a past lifetime as a man. While I pondered this, I noticed a gradual change in all my relationships. I got along better with everyone—even my mother. I began forming closer friendships. Still, I felt desperately lonely.

One day I was camping at a place called Horse Thief Lake. Ready to accept almost any answer to my

37

questions, I sat down to practice one of the Spiritual Exercises of ECK.

Suddenly it came to me. I realized I had been the very worst kind of thief possible—a thief of love.

I remembered I had been a minor monarch of a village in the dark ages, without a mate and very lonely. The quickest solution was the worst. I declared that everyone in the village must live alone until they found someone for me to marry.

This moment of awareness at the lake was a turning point for me.

After that, everyone who entered my circle of friends had the greatest luck finding a mate. Friends were getting married. Even friends of friends were planning their weddings. In this lifetime, everyone in my "village" had to get married first. Then I might get my turn.

Meanwhile, I needed to open my heart and let the love of God pour in. Divine, unconditional love surrounded me. I just had to learn to receive it.

Not worried about what I didn't have, I filled my heart with gratitude for all the love in my life. I gave thanks for my pet, my friends, a child's smile—even the fragrance of a flower. I had learned an important lesson. I didn't need a mate to feel loved. I was happier than ever before.

Finally, when I least expected it, the ECK, the Holy Spirit, brought me a wonderful husband. A friend for years, I could not accept him as my mate until I understood this lesson from my past life and learned how to truly recognize love.

10

Discovering Your Spiritual Purpose in This Life

Susan Sarback with Tim Bellows

When you ask a question from the heart, Divine Spirit answers. But It responds in Its own way, in Its own time.

For several months I had been wondering why we're here—about my own and others' spiritual missions. I asked the Inner Master, What can Divine Spirit teach me about that? One night, to my surprise, I received a simple message—as if someone were typing it in my heart: *Our mission and purpose in life is to love. Love ourselves, love God, love others, and love all of life.* I understood this as the basic, generic, mission for everyone.

Then the ECK, Divine Spirit, told me via the Inner Master, "There's a second kind of mission, your specific mission. It is your personal way to learn about love in this life. This personal mission may come in the form of a specific skill or life lesson."

I believe a personal mission is your individual way to feel and express God's love here and now. This ties in with a quote from *The Shariyat-Ki-Sugmad,* Book 2, the scriptures of Eckankar: "The aim and purpose of Eckankar has always been to take Soul by Its own path back to Its divine source."

So the road to God is not set! It's each Soul's job and responsibility to discover and follow Its own path home.

Divine Spirit has been generous in Its message to me, showing me that our mission is as close as our breath, as natural as our handwriting. In fact, it's so close that we often miss it.

We don't think it's much of anything.

Are you a natural-born singer? Gardener? Organizer? Family nurturer? It's interesting how many of us don't have a clue about the mission that is so much a part of ourselves.

Don't trip over your own gifts. They are your way of learning love and your way of serving life.

I've learned a wonderful spiritual equation: Doing what you love equals happiness. Happiness is living up to your high potential of becoming a Co-worker with God.

To put this into action, you may want to try a simple exercise: Take a piece of paper, and write down all the things you love. What makes you happy? Just brainstorm on paper for a few minutes—continue adding things over the next few days or weeks.

Then write down what keeps you from doing the things on your list. Take time to really contemplate and act on your discoveries.

What keeps us from finding our mission or from loving ourselves? First, we feel unworthy. We say, "I can't do it. I'm not good enough." Second, we don't listen. We have too many filters. We judge ourselves, thinking in terms of should and should not, good and bad, right and wrong. Or we have too many opinions about how things should be: "It's too hot to go out and paint." "It's too cold to stand out there and draw." "I'll have to drive to the store to get paints." These detours are experiences, our lessons, and as we learn to see a greater truth, they help us move into the divine consciousness.

A friend, Kathryn, has always cared for others—kids, older people, almost anyone with a need. She cooks for friends or cleans for them. Her nurturing qualities show in bold relief to most of us. In fact, she ended up working as a waitress for years and now manages restaurants, constantly serving others. And they love her for it. Her three children love her too!

I recently asked what her mission was. It surprised me that she didn't have a clue. She asked what *I* thought her mission was.

I answered, "It seems to me that your mission is to serve and care for others; that it's your way of living more fully and giving to life."

"I always suspected it might be caring for others," she laughed, "but because it was so easy and natural, I didn't think it was a very important mission."

The next thing that keeps us from finding our purpose and loving ourselves is procrastination. We continually say, "I'll get around to it sometime." But life flies by! Just ask any eighty-year-old person.

Another stumbling block can be not taking responsibility, not responding to our inner guidance. This block keeps life easy for us. Once we know our mission, we have to live it! This means commitment: less time to do other things and a lot more responsibility.

Some will commit to a mission as a karmic task. Another friend, Jim, found studying to be a doctor a breeze. He could skip many classes and still do exceptionally well on tests. He became a great doctor to whom other doctors turn for answers.

One day Jim and I had lunch. As we were catching

up on events in our lives, he gave me a book on Japanese warlords. I was shocked because just a few days earlier I had had a series of dreams and glimpsed a past life with Jim: He was a Japanese warlord who had killed thousands of people. This had hardly bothered him for he had not seen life as sacred then. I also saw in the dream that he had to be a doctor for many lifetimes after his Japanese warlord life. To learn the value of life, he had to be around those who are dying and try to heal them.

For Jim, his way of learning to love meant being a doctor. It was easy for him because of his bigger lesson—to learn the sacredness of life.

As Jim talked, he told me about a problem he had with his neck. It had become so severe he had almost died having surgery to fix the problem.

I realized that that fit perfectly; in my dream Jim used to eliminate his enemies by beheading them.

My own mission as an artist and teacher has proven to be an interesting road. I've known about it since childhood. Art was easy and natural, but I didn't want to take on the responsibility, the discipline I would need to express a pure state of consciousness on canvas.

I had to sacrifice many other activities to focus on art. Even though I loved it, it was a burden.

One day as I thought about art and teaching, I heard an inner message from Divine Spirit: "Your mission is your ticket home to God."

I realized my task was to be an artist and teach art. But my mission or lesson was to be receptive to the Holy Spirit, to refine my sensitivity, to learn about wonder and see the freshness in all life, and to appreciate the beauty in everything, seeing and knowing the rhythm of light. This was my way to love life more.

Several years after this realization, I again began to doubt myself. I still wasn't convinced. I was ready to give up my dreams of art and teaching. Then I had a dream where I met a man crouched in a dark, misty place. I knew I was meeting myself in a past life. This man had a mission: to tell me why I had to continue with art. He said, "L'amour est."

I was speaking to myself, as it were, in French— but in this life I don't know French!

I stopped at a library and couldn't find the meaning of the words. Finally I called a friend who speaks French. He told me that *l'amour est* means "Love is." So I had given myself the message from a past existence: Don't stay in the dark. Painting is your way to learn more about love and to give love.

For me, this path of living my love is the great ticket home to God.

And what is yours?

11

Striking a Bargain

David B. Oldham

*T*his was clearly a time of crisis.

As a labor representative for the local teachers' union, collective bargaining is my highest priority. A strike is the ultimate bargaining crisis. One Thursday afternoon I found myself representing one hundred and sixty-eight teachers beginning a strike.

That night I came down with the flu. Somehow I managed to make it through the next day at strike headquarters—the general meeting, the strategy sessions, the press releases, the scores of minicrises throughout the day.

By Friday night, I ached all over. All I could do was go home and drop into bed. Fevered and weak, I spent the entire weekend in bed. But I vowed to be well enough to go back to the bargaining table by Monday!

In the meantime I contemplated the spiritual meaning of this sudden illness. From my inner guidance, I saw that this flu was a reflection of my attitudes toward the group of teachers with whom I was working.

They were the toughest I had ever worked with. For months I had struggled to advise them about strategy and coax them through mediation. When they didn't heed my advice, I began to resent it.

My mistake was in allowing their resistance to

build up anger and resentment within me—resentment which I began to exhibit outwardly in times of stress. My fever was a manifestation of latent anger and frustration.

On the succeeding days of the strike, this understanding helped me to get a new point of view on the whole situation. I began to look at these teachers from a fresh perspective and to forget the anger of the past months. Each day was a new crisis for them, and I saw them as scared, uncertain people in a strange, new environment.

Just as I came to grips with that lesson regarding my anger, the next lesson was already building up momentum!

By Monday morning I was over the flu and back at strike headquarters—but now my lower back was killing me. There were pains shooting up and down my right leg.

I suffered through a strike-committee meeting, lunch with our attorney, and a meeting over insurance benefits for the striking teachers. That afternoon, I took my pain-racked body to the chiropractor to get my back adjusted.

By Monday night the pain was worse. I felt I would faint whenever I even got out of bed. I tossed and turned, trying to get comfortable enough to sleep.

Later that night I had a dream. In this dream I stood on a balcony overlooking a dungeon. I was dressed in Turkish robes. In the dungeon below, two guards held the arms of a prisoner. A third guard stood looming over the prisoner. In his raised hand was a gleaming curved sword—a scimitar—and he was aiming it right at the prisoner's lower back. While my Turkish wife turned away in grief, I commanded, "Execute him!" The sword fell and cut deeply into the man's spine.

I awoke immediately. I knew I had just witnessed a scene from a past life in which I had ordered an execution. I saw my current back problem as a karmic debt originating centuries ago in that Turkish dungeon.

This knowledge did not alleviate the pain, but at least I knew why I was suffering. I had to work out this condition once and for all. Meanwhile, the chiropractor's adjustments and a back brace allowed me to withstand the hours of mediation that were to follow.

Surprisingly, my physical frailty seemed to make the teachers see me more as a human being. From then on, we had more appreciation of each other and the problems we were working through. With this new level of trust, I was able to sit back and let them hammer out their own decision.

The strike was resolved when the teachers accepted a simple restructuring of the school board's original offer. By looking at the problem from another viewpoint, the perfect answer was found—one that had been there all along!

It turned out that physical therapy was required for healing my back. The therapist corrected my posture for sitting, driving, sleeping, getting out of bed, and getting up from a chair. As he worked, positive changes came into my habits and my outlook on life. While the therapist worked on realigning my physical body, I worked with the Mahanta on realigning my attitudes and my life!

I knew I was the woman, but who was this man? Someone urged me to move closer and be silent; the answers would come.

12
Dreaming My Life

Denise Naughton

Although dreams have always brought me spiritual insights, there are very few dreams I remember from my childhood. The ones I do remember woke me in the middle of the night, frozen with fear. Only the sound of my racing heart broke the silence.

These nightmares were very rare and always the same: My house was surrounded by Japanese warriors. I was the only defender against the onslaught of dozens. I would wake in a cold sweat just before they made their rush.

As I grew older, these dreams disappeared. But the key to unlocking their meaning surfaced years later in a love relationship.

From the beginning of our relationship, my partner and I enjoyed the easy familiarity of old friends. I remember once he mentioned he had known me a very long time ago. "How wonderful it is to be with you again," he said. I was taken aback by his comment. It was out of the ordinary for him and out of context with the conversation we were having.

I tried to quiz him, but he couldn't explain it. He seemed rather confused by what he had said. I knew it was a message from Divine Spirit, and I listened.

Our relationship was an unusual one. Everything seemed to indicate it would be long and full. However, we would reach a certain point and then, for no apparent reason, back away from each other. Every two to three years we reconnected, only to reach the same barrier again. This pattern repeated itself for almost twelve years.

During the years we were apart, our relationship continued in the dream state. My family and several of the ECK Masters of the Ancient Order of the Vairagi played a part in these dreams. My family was always confused: Why was I leaving such a wonderful man?

In other dreams our relationship grew in the ways I had always expected it to in my outer life. I was becoming very confused. Outwardly the relationship was going nowhere, but it was working so well on the inner!

One time after spending a few days with him, I returned home feeling inwardly beaten and broken.

Once again the wall of fear had reappeared. It reminded me of my childhood nightmares. A decision needed to be made: either I wanted us to be together completely—or not at all. But I was paralyzed. I couldn't decide what to do next.

I sat down and did a spiritual exercise to gain some insight into my fear and confusion. I asked the Mahanta, the Inner Master, to show me why I could neither shake this bond nor make it stronger. Then I fell asleep, and my dreams brought me the answers I sought.

In a dream that night I found myself in Japan. The setting was several centuries ago. I saw a woman and a man, both dressed in royal robes, their families attending. At first I thought I was watching a royal marriage, but then I realized the two were being slowly tortured.

Why? I knew I was the woman, but who was this man? Someone urged me to move closer and to be silent; the answers would come. Suddenly I found myself in the body of the woman I had been watching. My father was commanding me to deny the love I had for the man by my side. I asked him why. He replied that this man was the enemy of our family.

I replied he was no enemy of mine and turned to look into my lover's eyes. It was then that I recognized him as the man I knew in my present life. In this past life in Japan, he and I had died at a very young age at the hands of our own fathers. They had been lifelong enemies, coming together briefly for the murder of their only children.

When I awoke, I knew I had experienced a past life as Soul. All my childhood nightmares now made sense.

Those fears were gone—and with them, the bond with this man. I understood from the dream that our relationship could go no further in this lifetime. He would not be able to understand the obstacles we would have to overcome to renew our relationship as it was in that past life. But instead of feeling sorrow, I felt light and happy. I was walking away from this relationship with love, understanding why rather than resenting invisible circumstances.

Someday, I knew, this man and I would meet again on equal ground. This was the insight from my dream: that there is a love that is greater, freer, and stronger than the love I was familiar with in the physical world.

I could leave our relationship with love and know that it was still being healed on the inner planes.

Though the outcome of the relationship was not what I had visualized and hoped for, the ECK, or Holy Spirit, had given me something better: an open heart and an understanding I could carry with me forever.

13

Connections of the Heart

Coleen Rehm

The Eckankar Satsang class closed with the sound of a hushed HU-U-U, the love song to God. There was a moment of silence, then smiles everywhere. A tangible glow hung in the air. Through my peripheral vision, white light twinkled around each student. I wanted the moment to last forever.

People milled about the room, reluctant to depart. A group congregated near the door, trading hugs as they left. I quietly slipped into the outer foyer to be alone.

I saw another chela, a student of Eckankar— a person I'd spoken to barely half-a-dozen times before.

Shyly, I glanced at him as laughter from the other room trickled and spilled over us like water. His eyes met mine and a slow smile passed between us. Simultaneously, we laughed and shrugged, as if to say, Why not?

I extended my arms to him as he stooped slightly to surround me in a gentle hug. Closing my eyes as his arms clasped around me, I felt my heart open with a flood of warm light. I sensed his heart was open too, and it was as big as all outdoors.

Instantly, I saw a woman I knew to be myself, standing in an open meadow in front of a weather-beaten farmhouse. A prairie wind whipped her skirts as she gazed across distant fields, searching for the man she loved. A flash of recognition crossed her face.

Her wrinkles of worry melted into a smile as she ran into the arms of her husband. The warmth of their love enveloped them as they embraced.

As the vision faded from my inner eyes, I still felt those strong arms, wrapped with love around the prairie woman. With a start I realized—I knew this Soul! This was the man from the field. He was so familiar. I was struck wordless by the sacredness of the moment.

Slowly I grasped his shoulders and gazed into his soft, brown eyes. As he gazed back, I glimpsed something I'd seen in the eyes of wild animals. Pure ECK shone there, full of tenderness, trust, and the light of love. My breath caught in my throat. Tears sprang to my eyes as Soul acknowledged Soul. My heart overflowed with love.

"Get to know this chela better," the voice of the Inner Master said. Dimly, I heard the chela ask, "I'm going to grab a bite to eat. Care to join me?"

Inwardly I debated. I wanted to, but my ego fought for control. Incredulously, I heard my voice stammer out an apology. "Thanks, but some other time, maybe." I felt I wasn't ready for this experience. I wanted time to prepare—to be at my best.

Again, more insistently, I heard the Inner Master. "Get to know this chela, *now!*"

"I will, I will," I promised inwardly. "Later, just not right now." I turned hesitantly toward my car. An inner pull begged me to turn back. I stopped to look back, all the while inwardly kicking myself. Five minutes later, I found myself on the freeway, speeding home.

Days turned to weeks, and the weeks began to slip by, stacking into months. Still, my promise remained unfulfilled each time I saw the chela. Each time the Inner Master admonished, "There isn't much time. Get to know this chela."

Surely there must be plenty of time, I reasoned.

Finally I decided that at the upcoming Eckankar regional seminar I would be ready to get to know the chela. I counted on his attendance as a given fact—all the area ECKists planned to attend.

Strangely, the voice of the Inner Master was silent now. I felt alone, adrift without a guide. The Inner Master had no more words for me.

The seminar day arrived. My eyes scanned the crowd. I sought the familiar face of the chela, ready and eager to fulfill my promise. But the seminar passed without him.

Maybe he had been called out of town or caught a bad cold, I reasoned inwardly. The desire to fulfill my promise grew insistently stronger.

I spoke to a friend about the seminar the next day.

Casually, I asked if she had seen the chela. "Oh, Coleen." As she spoke, a funny look crossed her face.

"Didn't you know? He translated (died) nearly two weeks ago."

Anguish and regret welled up within me, and tears trickled down my cheek. I felt awkward and heavy—out of place. I had missed the opportunity to meet a new, old friend. But moreover, I'd broken my promise to the Inner Master and myself through neglect. This last realization hit me like a punch in the nose, and my face reddened.

"I heard but didn't listen," I cried inwardly. From that moment on, I vowed to have greater self-discipline. The words, "Trust your inner knowingness, live in the moment, and listen to the Inner Master," rang through my daily contemplations.

As I accepted the spiritual challenge, I felt my life imperceptibly speed up. Instinctively, I knew I was on a fast track to somewhere.

A week and a half later, it was my turn to open the ECK center. A fellow ECKist was moderating a class that evening. I found myself attracted to him in an inexplicably neutral way. Shortly thereafter, my vow to the ECK was tested. "Call him up and ask him out," I heard, "—but not yet." Moment by moment, I checked with the Inner Master as days passed. One afternoon, I felt a shift. "Now . . . call him *now!*"

Chanting HU inwardly, I found my attitude to be surprisingly neutral. This person was someone I'd like to know as a friend, nothing more. And if the ECK felt it a part of my journey to know this individual, then I was not one to argue.

The phone clicked, and his groggy voice traveled through the line, "Hello?"

"I'm sorry, did I wake you?" Amid apologies, I managed to stammer out who I was and an invitation to get together. Immediately my ego wanted to take it back and crawl into a hole. But Soul reigned, and a silence fell between us that couldn't have lasted even a minute, but felt like ten.

"Uh, yeah, sure, I guess so," he agreed. I wondered, had he checked on the inner too? I laughed inwardly, and in that moment I found the freedom to be myself. As time passed, we got to know each other better.

About six weeks later, during a quiet time together, I wondered what it would be like to be married to this guy. The next words out of his mouth were, "Will you marry me?" Instantly I asked the Inner Master, "What do I say?" and heard, "Say 'yes!'—if you want to."

I never imagined that the way to love could be

found by listening to the Inner Master, being true to myself, and living in the moment. But the Mahanta may use any experience along the journey to help the chela unfold.

14

A Debt Repaid—
Fifty Years Later

Geri Shanafelt

As with many important events in my life, working with the hospice program started as a coincidence.

My husband and I just happened to stop by a friend's house one Sunday afternoon. As we visited, she told me she was organizing a new hospice group in a neighboring county. She said that hospices are run by people who help the terminally ill patient who would rather die at home than in an impersonal hospital. I liked the philosophy.

Help is always needed in the home, she said. The hospice worker is on hand to lend a sympathetic ear, run errands, or give family members a break so they can leave the house for a while.

I decided then and there to volunteer my time and was immediately assigned to a woman in her seventies who was dying of lung cancer.

Generally, the first meeting between hospice worker and patient occurs in the home. But I remembered meeting this lady once before, when we had both adopted a puppy from the same litter. It was something to talk about in the beginning.

After a few hours she opened up a little and started telling me about her illness. The lung cancer wasn't a surprise. "When I had heart trouble," she said, "the doctor told me to stop smoking. Then I had leg problems, and the doctor again said, 'Stop smoking!' This time, when I couldn't breathe, I knew. I guess after three strikes, you're out."

As I left her home that day, I had a special feeling of warmth and love I could not explain. That night I had an interesting dream experience. The year was 1937. I was waiting, as Soul, for a physical body, but the woman aborted the pregnancy. When I awoke, I realized that the woman in my dream was my hospice patient. It had taken almost fifty years for me to meet her in the physical world.

The next day she confided (for whatever private reasons) that she had had an abortion in 1937. It was as close as she ever came to having a child. The materials for a baby quilt, which she had started to embroider all those years ago, had been neatly packed away in a suitcase. I was working on a quilt at the time, and this had sparked the conversation.

Suddenly she rose from her bed and pulled out a stack of beautifully stitched pieces of yellow cloth. "I don't know why, but I want you to have these," she said.

At that moment I knew that whatever karma had existed between us was now dissolved. Only love remained, from one Soul to another. She died several weeks later.

As a hospice volunteer, the relationships I have with patients are not always so clear. But hospice is a good way for me to share the love I receive each day during my ECK Spiritual Exercises, as I learn more about detachment, divine love, and the 360-degree overview of Soul.

15

Father Was Right After All

Gabriel Ezutah

y father was an interesting character. Humorous, wise, and gentle, he was not given to conventional religious thinking like many of his contemporaries. He often told me stories of how past lives influence present-life conditions.

He would paint the characters of my supposed previous incarnations so well that there was no room for doubts. I absorbed all he told me without question. Old and gray, but jovial and childlike, my father was my best friend.

Like most children, I had my fair share of childhood and adolescent illnesses. But my greatest problem was severe headaches, which attacked me two or three times a year.

My family tried all sorts of herbal and orthodox medications in an attempt to cure my headaches. My father would often spread his palms in utter helplessness and say, "This must be a carryover from your past life, my son." He would say it matter-of-factly without aiming to teach or convince. Maybe he was right; maybe he was wrong. Who cared whether there was a past-life connection if it did not make my headaches go away?

Then came Eckankar. Its teachings had so much in common with my father's philosophies that I didn't find them difficult to accept. I learned about HU, the ancient name of God, and sang it every day. I had some inner experiences that strengthened my spiritual convictions.

The most profound one came during another headache. The headache was so severe that I had to go to the hospital for the first time since my adolescence. The doctor gave me some injections and sent me home around 10:00 a.m. As I started down the stairs to a waiting car, my head started pounding, and I became dizzy. I tried to steady myself by grabbing the handrail, but I missed and fell down the short staircase, losing consciousness.

Around 11:00 p.m., I woke up in a hospital bed. I had malaria. For three days, in the intensive care unit, my condition continued to worsen. On the fourth night I was able to muster enough strength to sing HU for a while before falling asleep.

I awoke in a world of orange light. I felt free and without pain. I saw a bar and went in. Many people sat around tables, drinking beer and smoking heavily. They were all of European descent, and so was I. The room was filled with smoke. I searched for a vacant seat but could not find one. Although everybody looked familiar, none of them made any effort to acknowledge my presence. Feeling like an outsider, I decided to leave. I went through a door into the backyard and behold! There was Sri Harold Klemp, the Mahanta, the Living ECK Master.

I ran after him. As I reached out to touch the Master, a ball of yellow light blossomed from his radiant body and exploded before my eyes, enveloping me. Then I woke up, soaked with perspiration.

"This must be a carryover from your past life, my son!" My father's words echoed in my consciousness.

He was right. I suddenly realized my headaches had come from a lifetime of drinking and smoking in excess. The ball of yellow light from the Mahanta was an experience in the Light and Sound of God intended to open my eyes to the truth. My dream was a vivid spiritual wake-up call.

Eckankar teaches about past lives and reincarnation as well as the freedom of Soul. But a past-life recall is important only if it helps to heal the present. And this is possible through the help of the Mahanta, the Living ECK Master. Surprisingly, I had this spiritual encounter a full six months before I became a member of Eckankar.

I no longer drink or smoke. I have not had one headache since my dramatic dream encounter with the Inner Master. Father was right after all.

16

No Fear of Dying

Ben Hunter

*I*n 1979 I had a dream within a dream which changed my view of death overnight. At the time I was very unhappy and wanted nothing more than to run my life into the ground and be done with it.

In the midst of this despair, I was given a book on Eckankar written by Paul Twitchell which was the only light in my otherwise darkened world.

After reading the book I had this dream—if truly it can be called such, for I have no recall of falling asleep that night. As soon as I lay my head on the pillow, I stepped into the midst of another life.

I could recall another childhood with different siblings and a complete set of memories, hopes, and dreams leading to that present moment. I was in the intelligence branch of the British Army, in World War II. Crowds surged in the streets as I hurried unnoticed down the less-crowded back roads to a prearranged rendezvous.

Climbing the stairs of the appointed building, my thoughts turned to the recent events of the war. I was vitally interested in what new strategy would be laid before me behind the closed door ahead. But when I saw their plan, I was speechless with anger. I was to impersonate an enemy informant in a meeting with a key Nazi officer. It was madness, for I knew the officer was far too familiar with the man I would impersonate to be taken in. But I had no choice. I had my orders and would fulfill them the best I could.

When I arrived the next day in the clearing that was our appointed meeting place, the officer was waiting for me with a dozen armed escorts. As I approached, our eyes locked, and immediately I realized that he knew I was an impostor. I turned and fled. His soldiers gave chase as he barked commands.

I ran for the woods on a small path covered with pine needles. As I crested a small rise, I tripped and fell, protected momentarily by the hill. I had no time to think, however, as bullets flew.

I jumped up and whirled to face my attackers, who were less than forty yards away. Two soldiers fired simultaneously, rifles clutched to their hips, striking me in the stomach and chest. As I fell, I began to leave that body. Then my viewpoint shifted back to the ground for a moment. As I looked out of the eyes, I saw only the ground all around me. But at the same time I was aware of an overview, as if this whole forest were the stage of a theater and I was the director peering down from above.

I felt the footsteps of an approaching soldier and watched from above as the commander directed him to finish me off. He placed the barrel of his rifle under my right armpit and pulled the trigger.

The bullet dove into my body like a diver through multicolored waters, taking my consciousness with it. All else was gone now, as image after image hurtled by: Queen Victoria, regiments in red coats, lives in Rome, Greece—back further and further in time until finally there was only a stream of orange-and-yellow-and-gold light.

I finally came to rest. First, in a place where I seemed to be lying on black rocks by a black ocean with the waves pounding me under a black sky. Then this too faded, until I was only a thin line of beingness stretched from here to there, with no thought in between but the feeling of lying on my back and on my stomach, on the ceiling and the floor—all at the same time; none more than the other.

There was no body and no thought; no images to grasp, but still there was beingness. Then there came a twist, a snapping of this thin line of consciousness that sent a ripple the length of my universe. I wanted nothing more than to remain in this place, but this was not to be. As the impulse rolled through my being, I moved with it and was sent spiraling down, back toward the human state of consciousness.

I awoke with a start and sat straight up in bed, drenched with sweat. The shock waves continued to roll through me as I became—as if for the first time—the person I am now. The experience, and the expansion of consciousness it brought, was too great to hold in my human awareness.

Overwhelmed, I got up and headed for the bathroom. As I walked shakily down the hall, my brother poked his head out of the next room. He rubbed his face sleepily, but his gaze was sharp as he asked, "You OK?"

"I guess so," I said. "Go back to sleep." He shambled back to bed, and I returned to mine.

Now I entered another state. The next thing I knew, I was again suddenly awakening in bed with the first experience of awakening vividly impressed on my mind. As I reviewed each scene, it all began to feel more like a dream—until I came to the sequence with my brother. Then a tingle went up my spine. My brother was not next door, but thousands of miles away in northern Africa.

I knew then that I could never cease to exist. Death was only a transition from one life to another and could provide no escape from this life. Whatever problems I faced would surely follow me, life after life, until I worked them out as Soul.

As I sat quietly in bed, I became aware of Paul Twitchell looking at me from the inner planes as the dawn broke over the tops of the trees outside my window. The book on Eckankar I had read was still on my nightstand.

You see, his look seemed to say, this is the way it is.

And I did see. With the fear—and hope—of death removed, there was nothing to do but get on with life and solve its mysteries.

A parade of past lives was shown as the dream continued. In one of the past lives, I saw myself as an operatic singer with a successful, international career.

17

A Trip to the Mental Plane

Jean Louise Lindahl

I am an operatic singer. When I sing, the sound surges through my body, my instrument. The vibrations make me feel like a crystal about to break. It is an exquisite feeling.

The downside—so often portrayed in the media—is a sensitive, artistic temperament. An artist can feel things intensely and translate the human experience to others through music, art, writing, or theater. My question was, How does an artist maintain balance?

Lately, I'd been facing some stormy waters psychologically, and my dream life reflected it. I felt I needed balance, something stronger than the usual dream experiences to ferry me over these rough seas.

Then I discovered a brief reference in an Eckankar publication about a clinic for healing on the Mental Plane. That very night before falling asleep I asked to visit the Mental Plane and receive a healing session at the clinic.

The next morning I awoke feeling lighter, as if a heavy burden had been removed. But I had no conscious recollection of any dream experience. I was grateful for whatever had occurred during the night, but I knew my problem hadn't disappeared. I wanted and needed more in-depth work, so I kept asking to go

71

to the clinic. For two more weeks I asked and yet had no recall of being there.

Finally the Dream Master drew back the curtain of my resistance, and one morning I awoke with the following, intensely vivid dream experience fresh in my mind:

I dreamed I was given the name of a doctor. Above all else, I wanted to be certain that he was the right doctor for me. I skeptically called him on the telephone. The more we talked, the more I relaxed. Soon I was convinced that he was someone I could trust. In the dream, I made an appointment to see him in person.

I eagerly arrived at the appointed time, filled with hope and expectation. The room was filled with therapists, the doctor, and four nurse-assistants. Through various methods they began to reveal qualities about my inner nature that were incredibly accurate. I was amazed at the sophistication of their diagnostic techniques.

I had the strong impression that these therapists had lived through the same inner struggle I now encountered. They had themselves proceeded through a healing analysis and emerged whole. Now, in turn, they were treating others struggling with the same dilemma.

After these preliminary realizations, the real work began. They revealed my own nature to me, aspect after aspect. At one point, I tried to retreat from the acute pain of self-realization and felt a fog fill the room. The fog had a remarkable source; it was issuing from my own eyes! I strove to look through it, to see again, and I felt the fog gently lift.

A parade of past lives was shown as the dream continued. In one of the past lives, I saw myself as an operatic singer with a successful, international career.

I had carried my inner urge to its fullest expression and lived the artistic life I had always aspired to. But I couldn't understand why so many things in my present lifetime stood in the way of attaining this once again.

Two burning questions imprinted themselves on my mind: What is the relationship between the artistic/creative person and psychological imbalance? And if my aberrations are removed, will I retain my artistic abilities?

When I asked them about this, the therapists laughed and laughed. But they were kind enough to answer my hungry mind: The weaknesses would go, my talents would stay—only now, they would be more free than ever before to manifest.

Though I felt I had learned a lot, the session was not over yet. The therapists kept revealing more, until the realizations became finer, deeper, more piercing. I felt myself slipping, losing consciousness. The therapists handled this deftly, and I felt them gently bring my attention into focus.

As I slowly came back, they applied pressure to the exact point where the acute realization and pain originated. They used a technique somewhat like acupressure. As they pressed the point, the energy centered there was released and dissipated like fog.

In the dream I realized why for years I had carried a quote by Felix Mendelssohn in my wallet: "God, art, and life are but one."

I'd come back again in this lifetime to take that philosophy one step further: Art is but a step on the long, well-traveled path back to God.

As I was released from the pain of centuries, I left the inner clinic, understanding this was the first of a series of sessions that were a part of my spiritual healing.

I awoke from the dream with lingering, vivid memories and a deep gratitude regarding what had occurred. I felt a renewed desire to face life directly again, without fear. What an incredible gift from the Mahanta!

18

An Important Decision

Ingrid Haller

As I flew home from the ECK European Seminar that year, my heart was still closed from the emotional difficulties in my life. The seminar hadn't lifted the heaviness. Most of the hour-and-a-half flight back to Zurich I spent in the airplane's bathroom, sick from what I later learned was food poisoning.

I spent the next five days in bed; the pills the doctor had prescribed didn't help. My weight dropped dramatically in those five days as my condition worsened. I became so weak I could barely walk to the bathroom.

My life was miserable; I was disappointed in everything. I knew what I needed most was love, but I didn't understand anything about it. During this time, my mate brought me food and drink, but he let me go through my difficulties alone. One day he came in the room and said firmly, "You have to decide whether you want to die or live!"

This shocked me because I hadn't realized I was letting myself slip into such a deep depression that it could end my life. His comment snapped me out of my apathy, and I called a friend who is an ECKist and a medical doctor. She said to go back to the hospital.

During the next five days, I stayed in a strange semiconscious state, not aware if I was alive or dead.

For a while, I seemed to be watching many television screens. On each screen was an image of myself, pictures from this life and past lives. Most were hard to accept.

These screens stayed in my vision whether my eyes were open or closed. Every time I had an emotional reaction to what I saw on a screen, I would feel a horrible pain in my stomach. This forced me to be neutral, to learn how to see myself from Soul's point of view and not to react to myself with hatred anymore.

After a time, the many TV screens faded to just one. I began to watch the absorbing drama of one of my past lives in detail. I was a Catholic nun of about thirty, the same age as I was now, in this life. I was on my deathbed. A circle of six to eight nuns stood around me. They were all very kind and loving.

All at once I was lifted out of the nun's body. I could suddenly see what kind of medicine would save my life.

I returned to consciousness and asked the nuns to go look for this medicine. They refused kindly and with sweet smiles, saying that it was not fitting with Catholic ways to use the herbs. I felt terrible anger, knowing I would die because of their spiritual ignorance.

Next, I fell into light sleep and had an important dream: Many ragged men were stumbling out of a glacier. They were bleeding and their ghastly screams rent the air as they ran in all directions. The men were shouting that they had been buried for forty years.

When I awoke, I knew the men symbolized my own pain and emotional hurts. They had been frozen in my being before this life even began. Now they were coming to the surface to be healed.

Soon after, a man dressed in gray came to me while I was in a half-sleep. He had a gray face, beard, and aura. I was very weak but instinctively turned my back to him. Later I realized that he was the Angel of Death. In turning my back, I had decided to live.

Over the next few weeks, I rested and sorted through my dramatic healing experiences. As a child, my mother had tried to tell me about her Christian beliefs. I always wondered why I was the only one of her three children who refused to hear anything about it. Each time I stepped into a Christian church, a feeling of great sadness would come over me, forcing me to leave. Now I understood why.

I knew that in my life as a Catholic nun I had started to work my way back home to God. But that life was cut short and ended in bitter disappointment that carried over into this life. It kept me searching until I was led to the truth of the Mahanta, the spiritual guide who could take me into the deeper secrets of love.

When I revisited the experience of dying in that life, I discovered with a shock that one of the nuns around my bed then is a family member in this life. We'd always had difficulties and fights. Now our relationship is slowly healing. She too is starting to seek a deeper meaning in life.

In this experience the Mahanta helped me heal my emotional body from the afflictions of anger and a poor self-image that had held me back in this life. Now I am much happier and lighter as I pursue my understanding of giving and accepting love and how the ECK, Divine Spirit, works in daily life.

19

Parent Lake

Mary Carroll Moore

I've always been uneasy about being alone in the wilderness, even though it pulls me with its intense beauty. My childhood summers were spent canoeing lakes in the Adirondacks where my grandmother owned a summer camp. Living in Minnesota, about six hours' drive from the Boundary Waters wilderness area, I imagined, with pleasure, paddling remote lakes under cloudless skies.

Yet behind this desire to enjoy nature at its most untamed was a persistent sense of its lurking danger.

Several summers ago my husband and I started packing for our first canoe trip. I was blissfully unaware how my underlying unease had gotten hold of our planning, but it began to show in the heaps of food I wanted to bring. Nothing seemed enough. Every trip to the store brought home more freeze-dried packages, another bag of fruit or candy bars, a couple more boxes of emergency rations.

The pile grew in a corner of my living room—more than a week's worth of rations for a family of five.

Driving north that weekend was a gentle process of shedding the familiar cities and sights. We passed patchwork fields and neat farmlands, going deeper into the unknown territory of the wilderness. We stopped to visit farm stands and eat in a roadside restaurant.

The day was warm and pleasant, and the bright blue canoe shone on the roof rack in the sunlight.

As we neared the wilderness that afternoon, I grew drowsy and lethargic, lulled by the gentle sounds of the car. In my half-sleep, the scent of the pine woods filled the air, and a strange dream crossed my vision.

* * *

I stood in a sunlit forest clearing, dressed in greasy buckskin, the tight loop of a beaded band on my upper arm. I knew I was alone, and it frightened me very much. A tight band also gripped my heart; for some reason I knew I must be very quiet. The name Monegwa *came to mind.*

* * *

The car jolted, and I woke suddenly, a cold, constricted feeling in my chest.

We arrived at Snowbank, the first lake, toward evening. Our plan was to spend the night at a shoreside campsite, then portage the canoe to a second, more remote lake the next morning. But I convinced my husband to push on, in the few hours of light left in the summer evening.

I made it sound easy: a relaxed paddle to the portage trail, maybe a mile to carry our gear and canoe, then another lake to cross as the sun set behind the trees.

The remote lake is Parent, isolated and accessible only by air, paddle, or foot.

As we loaded the canoe, I joked about the abundant food supplies, then silently added more packages to the space beneath my canoe seat, not sure why it was so important but wishing I'd brought even more. We set off across Snowbank, enjoying the slanting rays of evening light and the sound of other canoeists in the distance. When we reached the portage trail on the far side, we discovered the canoe was too heavy with supplies to lift out of the water, so we unloaded it and began carrying the first of many boxes and bags up a root-strewn dirt trail that led to Parent Lake.

My first glimpse of Parent Lake gave me an unexpected shock. It looked eerie in the setting sun, a bank of dark clouds casting an almost greenish light over the surface.

Much rougher than Snowbank, the water was thrashed by a sharp wind that caused the waves to lap aggressively against the rocky shoreline. Our paddles pushing through the water like heavy spoons in molasses, we slowly worked our way across the rough lake. The shoreline, studded with deformed pines and ravaged by the wind, hung dark shadows over the lake's surface in the twilight.

It seemed to take forever to reach our campsite, and as we pulled the canoe onto the rocky beach, I was again overcome by an almost incapacitating drowsiness and great sadness.

What was going on?

The uncomfortable feelings paralyzed me until I was unable to perform the simplest task, even unpacking a pot to boil water for tea. The sun was setting rapidly now, and I sat hunched on a fallen log while my husband set up the tent and started the cooking fire. The feeling that overcame me, shutting out all others, was that I would die soon, in this place, and no one would know.

The stupor continued through the evening. That night, before I fell into a light sleep, I listened for a long time to a pair of loons calling, laughing, across the lake.

The comforting sound counteracted the deep sadness I felt and relaxed my heart. I seemed to remember someone I loved telling me a story about loons—God's gentlest birds—protecting the frail beings in this world. I drifted to sleep listening to their almost-human cries and smelling the strong piney scent of the trees that encircled the clearing.

* * *

In my dream I am again Monegwa, and I am sitting on a fallen log, stiff with misery. I have walked all day to this remote clearing on the shore of a small lake. I am very far from my home territory, which is good because my parents want to kill me. I have observed them commit a heinous crime against the tribe. They have lied to the elders, and I am blamed. My grandmother has secreted me out of the camp at night, taking me to a trail that stretched into the distance.

Seven years old, hardly a man, I must go into the wilderness alone and try to survive.

Sitting in the clearing surrounded by pines, I remember my grandmother's parting words. She has told me to listen for the loon, the bird of laughter and joy, my protector in this life. The loon, she says, will remind me that there are those in the tribe who still love me. Leaving her I feel great sadness, and fear pulls at my heart. The harsh beauty of the wilderness offers me little comfort.

Because I am weak with sadness and unable to stir myself to find food or make a fire, I die in the clearing a few days later.

* * *

The dream was only a faint memory as we packed up early the next morning and paddled away from the pine clearing on the shore of Parent Lake. The further we went, the better I felt. Our canoe glided swiftly over the now-glassy water, and the portage trail was sunlit and mostly downhill. The first thing I heard when we arrived at Snowbank was the clear, happy sound of children's laughter echoing from a nearby cove.

You go along in life, and you may have a problem or a feeling you don't understand. It's often irrational and out of proportion to present life. If the window opens on a past life that caused the problem, you may have a chance to gain a broader perspective. Then you can learn the lesson and get on with your life today, released from one more bond with the past.

The window that opened on Monegwa's life and death at Parent Lake didn't fully erase my unease with being alone in the wilderness. I simply have more peace now with unexplained emotions. When they come, I know that fighting them is not the answer. I stay aware of the situation, try to surrender, maybe get some sleep, or do a Spiritual Exercise of ECK to gain perspective. Sometimes I get an inner cue to take action to realize the meaning of the problem.

After a time, there is usually a healing, and happiness comes again in the present moment.

20

How to Find Freedom from Yourself

Harold Klemp

What do you suppose makes people unhappy? A survey would probably list a hundred reasons, both real and imagined.

Now how many of those people do you think would like to hear the true reason for their unhappiness? Just a guess—very few.

The choices you've made in the past are the direct cause of all your unhappiness today.

If this answer doesn't suit you, don't read another word. You have better things to do. But maybe you're one of the few people who doesn't absolutely reject the above explanation for your unhappiness. Then keep reading. Perhaps you'll see *how* and *why* individuals make bad choices.

Most important, you may learn how to stop making them.

Let's start with a few examples of how poor decisions in past lives contributed to one person's lack of freedom and unhappiness in this lifetime.

We'll call her Shelley to insure her privacy. Shelley knows about karma. It's a repayment, or balancing of books, for our past misdeeds, but also for acts of generosity. Old missteps cause us pain today. On the other hand, past generosity to others is the reason for any happiness that offsets the pain. The balance between them makes life more bearable.

Shelley does the Spiritual Exercises of ECK every day. So the Mahanta, the Inner Master, showed her three earlier lives to provide an insight into her grapplings with misplaced worth and identity in relation to others.

In short, these three past lives left her feeling worth less than other people. That attitude has caused her a lot of agony in this lifetime.

Here follows a brief summary of three of her earlier lives.

• Past Life Number 1

She calls the first past life "The Vanity Queen" lifetime.

Shelley was a queen then, a woman of power, influence, and beauty in a long-ago time and place. She gave her attendants shabby treatment—as some people in power do—while her attendants lavished care upon her. Her slightest wish was their command.

Her designers lived to dress her, a beautiful and striking woman. *God must have a reason for giving me this beauty,* she thought.

On top of that, God had also given her much intelligence in the popular sense. A good sense of intuition rounded out her arsenal. It made her believe she could outthink people most of the time, and she used all these inner talents to protect her ego. A sad abuse of power.

In looking back at that lifetime, Shelley realized that all mistakes then, subtle and glaring, were embedded in her own choices.

A spirit of charity would have been easy. God had given her many advantages, and there were countless goods at her disposal to share with others. But she was stingy when it came to acts of generosity and charity. They had to be her idea. She refused to give help when others needed or expected it on the grounds that it would sacrifice her freedom of choice.

Shelley was the darling of the times, but she was like a spider in the bed.

The Mahanta let her see that her choices were those of immaturity and selfishness over love. Shelley had hardly made wise choices.

In this lifetime, she realizes the great debt she owes her dear parents, once helpless subjects of her abuse and neglect. The Mahanta, the Inner Master, would reveal to her the consequences of such immaturity and wretched behavior during two later lifetimes.

The Law of Karma then came into play. Shelley lost the opportunity to choose, even to the point of losing the right of her own opinions.

• Past Life Number 2

Next, the Mahanta let her revisit a lifetime in which she was the mistress of a low-level political appointee. He was only a remote member of a royal family that was in power hundreds of years ago. A nobody.

Yet he provided her well with material goods. There were plenty of fine clothes and an abundance of food.

In return, he got a beautiful consort. She had an ageless, childlike face with big eyes, full lips and cheeks, and shiny golden brown hair that rippled like a river of light. Her owner prized her above all other women, so she never faced the threat of replacement. But people around her regarded her as one might luncheon meat.

They never let her forget their scorn.

It left her with feelings of low worth—mentally, emotionally, and spiritually—right into the present lifetime.

That sheltered life was one in which she lacked power of any sort. From birth she was unequal. She accepted her lot with loneliness and vacancy. Unable to even control her own beauty, she was only a plaything for her owner.

• Past Life Number 3

The Mahanta then opened her vision to the next lifetime. It was another echo of that first life, even as the second had been. Again, with some power returned to her by the Lords of Karma, she ended up making more poor choices.

Reincarnated as a male, she joined the church around the time of the Inquisition. She rose quickly in the hierarchy due to her obedience to church disciplines and an absolute commitment to the letter of the law. Her lack of imagination was evident, but it was amply rewarded by her strict obedience to church law. Soon, she was a full participant in the Inquisition.

She loved to torture victims. Their cries could not touch her heart, because she had few feelings of her own. Shelley was perfect for the job. Only the church had value. Unmoved by human suffering, she was an ideal machine for the evils of the time.

So in this lifetime, Shelley's been sickened by man's inhumanity to man—the least of her troubles from her cruelty to others then.

Most of those past-life debts are paid up, thanks to all the help from the Mahanta, the Living ECK Master and the Spiritual Exercises of ECK. Her obligations to her parents, among others, are nearly all in balance now. These lessons from the past have taken her from spiritual immaturity to divine love.

The fast lane to freedom can be yours, too, in Eckankar.

Part Two

Dreams

Daydreams, night dreams, contemplation, Soul Travel—all are steps in the pursuit of heaven. In Eckankar, the student is under the protection of a spiritual guide known as the Mahanta.

21

Dreams, Your Road to Heaven

Harold Klemp

Our dreams are the forgotten road to heaven. This was once a nearly absolute truth. That is, until the teachings of ECK surfaced in 1965 to encourage people to look for the lost doorway between heaven and earth: their dreams.

Dreams are the starting point for many who wish to begin the spiritual journey to God and do it in the easiest possible way.

There simply is no better way to start than with our dreams. Good works may carry us far along this holy journey, and prayer is indeed a boon, but generally we can learn more about the true nature of God through the secret knowledge of dreams.

Daydreams, night dreams, contemplation, Soul Travel—all are steps in the pursuit of heaven. In Eckankar, the student is under the protection of a spiritual guide known as the Mahanta. This is the Spiritual Traveler, the Dream Master.

As the Mahanta, he is the Inner Master, the one who comes on the inner planes to impart knowledge, truth, and wisdom. But he also has an outer side. Here he is known as the Living ECK Master. Thus, the

spiritual leader of Eckankar can work both inwardly
and outwardly with all who come to learn of God and
life.

Once he requests it, a person who travels in his
dream worlds is assured of the Mahanta's protection.
This is helpful because in those lower heavens that lie
between earth and the true worlds of God, there are
shady people who like nothing better than to cheat or
harm innocent victims.

In Africa, for instance, the power of black magic is
very strong. An African man reported a dream in which
a group of men and women took him to a high place.
Unknown to him, these people were warlocks and
witches. When they reached the top of this place, which
was a towering seawall, a woman in the group told him
to jump into the sea. But he knew that all who jumped
from that height never came back.

"Jump!" she urged. As if hypnotized, he began to
move toward the edge of the wall. At that moment, the
Mahanta appeared. The group vanished. The Master
smiled and patted the dreamer on his shoulder; then
the dreamer awoke.

What few would recognize is that the Mahanta
prevented the dreamer's death. It often happens that
a dreamer who does not have the protection of the
Mahanta simply dies in his sleep. The doctor writes off
the cause as heart failure or some other physical condition. Often as not, however, the dreamer had wandered beyond the safe limits of his inner world and met
a psychic criminal, who was responsible for his death.
An experience that did not have to be, had he known
of the Mahanta, the Living ECK Master.

Dreams are one road to heaven. Another way to
enter is through contemplation: a few minutes each
day of spiritual relaxation in which the individual sits

with his eyes closed and sings the holy name of God. This word is *HU*. The Inner Master comes, in time, to take him into the worlds of heaven, the Far Country. With the Master along, what may otherwise have been a nightmare turns out to have a spiritual end.

In the following instance, the Mahanta was the guide for an ECK initiate during an experience in contemplation.

The Master took her to a large white-domed temple with stately pillars. In front of the temple was an enormous Buddha made of iron—the temple's guardian. He was seated on a circular platform.

"Bow down and worship me!" he commanded.

Awed by this thirty-foot-tall entity, she immediately began to prostrate herself before him. But the Master said, "We don't worship this entity." To the Buddha, he said, "I just want to show her something of interest down the left corridor." The Buddha blinked his massive eyes once, very slowly, in approval. The way was clear for them to enter the temple and for her to learn the secret wisdom of ECK which was stored there.

More often, though, we start our study of heaven through dreams. They are a most natural way. The student of ECK finds that his dreams become ever more spiritual as he continues his search for God.

The mind is the chief obstacle in the search for God. It tries to have the dreamer forget dreams in which the Mahanta imparts divine wisdom. So the Master must bypass this wall created by the mind.

One way the Mahanta, the Living ECK Master accomplishes this is seen in a dream study by a member of Eckankar. When the Mahanta wanted to remind her to avoid gossip and honor the Law of Silence, she had a dream in which something unpleasant was in her mouth. When the Master's lesson was on the "play" of life, her dream experiences dealt with school, group meetings, clubs, dorms, households, even pageants. When it was necessary for her to recall travel through higher levels of consciousness, her dreams were of stairs, steps, elevators, mazes of rooms, and even of herself on a child's swing.

Dreams are a road to heaven. They are not the only road; they do not go straight to the highest heaven, but they do offer a sound beginning for anyone who sincerely wants to find God.

In ECK, we are familiar with dreams of past lives. Other dreams give us insight into our health, family concerns, love interests, business plans, and guidance in how to live our lives with minute-to-minute care, if we are interested in developing our study of dreams to such a degree.

But the most important dream category is the spiritual dream. It tells us something about our present life, with all its struggles.

We learn about hidden motives, which most people wish to leave undisturbed in the dark corners of their minds.

Here is a spiritual dream, so that when you have one you have a measure to compare it with.

A dreamer awoke in her dream to find herself alongside the ocean. A high mound of sand ran parallel to the water, like a breakwater. She noticed she was on the side nearest the ocean. Looking closely at the mound of sand, she found little booklets buried in it and picked one up. An ECK Master came and read the message in the booklet for her.

"You've won a white used car," he said.

Used? She pulled another booklet from the mound, hoping for a message that said she had won a new white car. Instead, the ECK Master read: "You've won $113,000 in groceries." A second before she awoke, she found herself on the other side of the mound, away from the ocean.

The spiritual meaning came to her loud and clear: She had taken a step backward in her spiritual life. It came as a shock to her to see how attached she had become to worldly things. Only a month earlier she had written a two-word letter to the Living ECK Master: "I'm ready." She meant, for a higher state of consciousness.

This dream was a humbling experience. She now realized that the Mahanta had given her the used car in the dream because it was right for her at the time. It was the Master's gift, no matter how "used" it may have seemed to her. The next gift was a credit for spiritual food. She was thus able to take a new look at herself, honestly. From that dream she was then able to move up spiritually as she had desired.

Many more stories could be told about dreamers who have been enriched by their dreams. The study of dreams is an art, a highly interesting spiritual endeavor. It gives deep satisfaction to all who wish to learn more about themselves through personal experience.

Above all, dreams are of priceless spiritual worth to us, because they open our personal road to heaven.

22
Blinding Blue Light: Miracle in the Operating Room

Carol Kaminski

One February, I lost my sister to AIDS. She was very interested in Eckankar at the end of her life. After years of drug use and hard experiences, she embraced the fact that we are responsible for our lives. As Soul, we each make spiritual choices every day. She began to listen to my descriptions of the Spiritual Exercises of ECK, of how they help us find our highest destiny, and of how, as divine Soul, we choose our lessons.

I was very saddened by her death. But soon after, life began tugging me out of my grief, with the news that my first child would be born the following March.

A month or so before the due date, I met my sister in the dream state. Somehow I knew we were walking the streets of London, England. I was surprised to see my spiritual guide, the Mahanta, walking with her— and that my sister was carrying my baby in her arms.

"Do you know the Mahanta too?" I asked her in the dream.

"Oh, yes," she replied, "I walk with him now. But that's not why I'm here. I've been chosen to deliver a message to you. They picked me, someone you're familiar with, so you wouldn't be too afraid."

My sister looked me full in the eyes. "You're going to have your baby soon. It's going to be a traumatic experience. You will have to have a cesarean, but don't be scared."

"No, I'm not!" I exclaimed. "I'm having my baby naturally."

"No, it's not going to be what you expect," my sister insisted. "It's going to be scary, but very special. You'll have a sign that everything is going to be OK. Both you and the baby will live."

Suddenly, my circumstances struck me as odd. "Well, it's getting late," I told my sister, "and I can't be out on the streets of London. I'm pregnant! I should get back to my husband."

Before I could turn away, she thrust the swaddled baby into my arms. It was a boy.

As the dream faded, I realized that in my conscious mind, I didn't know the sex of the baby. My husband and I had asked not to know when they did my sonogram tests. I awoke in a sweat. But wait! It was more than sweat—my water had broken!

Within minutes, I was in the hospital. The baby was in breech position (backward in the womb), and suddenly everything deteriorated. They couldn't turn the baby, the umbilical cord was prolapsing, and a cesarean was needed.

The doctor told me he couldn't knock me out, and the next two hours were a panic of crying and screaming. I was afraid, my husband was afraid, and then finally the doctor told me even he was nervous. The baby and I were both in danger.

Things had reached a crossroads. Time was of the essence. I managed to breathe out, "This is it—such pain—can I sing my special song, the HU?"

One of the doctors said, "Lady, please! Do anything you can! I don't care what it is—we need all the help we can get here."

I started to sing HU with my husband as loud as I could, as several doctors and nurses continued their work.

The next thing I knew, the baby was born. All during my pregnancy, I had asked Divine Spirit if I could witness Soul, my baby, enter Its physical body. And at the moment when they held the tiny body of my little boy up, a blinding light rushed through the room.

It cut a swath in the shape of a huge, neon-blue Z. (A blue light is often a sign of the guidance and protection of the Mahanta, who is known inwardly by the name Wah Z.) Then the light landed in the baby's body—and he cried out with life. The nurses looked stunned as they wrapped him up. When I was handed my son, I realized he appeared just as he had in my dream with my sister, all swaddled up.

I looked into his face. He smiled, and a moment of profound peace came over me.

Then the doctors and nurses gathered around and told me he was a very special and lucky baby. "Whatever that HU business was that you were doing, it was really something," one said.

"Why do you say that?" I inquired.

"Well," he admitted, "I don't know if you all saw it, but the light in the OR turned blue!"

"Did you see that too?" another one exclaimed.

The next day they each came to my room individually, to ask more about the HU. My Chinese anesthesiologist kept saying, "Do the HU for me. This HU—it helped you, it saved the baby, and it saved me too! This is the thing to do!"

Most of the nurses just accepted the amazing blue light as a sort of special sign. But it bothered a couple of the doctors. They asked around to see if the power had gone off, causing the generators to kick in. But nothing unusual had happened with the electrical system of the hospital that day.

A few of my medical attendants even asked shyly if they could visit the Eckankar center. They also posed funny questions like, "Did you have any connections with anything electrical before you came into the OR?" I just smiled, as they recounted the story of the day the operating room turned blue.

Only when I returned home did it dawn on me. My baby was born on the very day that I lost my sister— a year later to the day. She proved to me that death is just another step in the circle of Soul's existence.

23

Dreaming on the Job

Randy Ward

*R*ecently, for the first time in my fifteen years as a building contractor, I got a paper cut from a set of plans I was working with. It barely caught my attention until it happened again, not just twice, but three times.

One of the ways Divine Spirit speaks to us is through the little events of daily life, but we have to pay attention. In Eckankar, we call these experiences waking dreams. When I pay attention, it doesn't take three tries to reach me, but when I'm busy or under stress, sometimes Spirit has to keep trying.

After mulling over the repeated paper cuts, I recognized that they were telling me to cut my bid for the job I was bidding on. *My price is already as low as I can go!* I argued to myself. But the nudge persisted. I decided to ask my spiritual guide, the Mahanta, to show me how to lower the bid—and still stay in business!

That evening, I did a spiritual exercise before drifting off to sleep. I silently asked the Mahanta how I could lower this bid.

That night I dreamed that my foreman was working on a job. I noticed he was doing all the work himself, so I pitched in to help him. When I awoke and wrote the dream in my dream journal, I realized I had received my answer. I could perform some of the manual labor myself. This would allow me to lower the bid. I did this, and we got the job.

I've been a student of dreams in Eckankar for over two years now. This experience demonstrated to me in a very real way how the guidance and love of the Holy Spirit and the Mahanta come to us in both the waking and sleeping states to help us smooth out the rough spots of life.

24

Thank You for Saving My Baby!

Adebayo Y. Olaomo Amusat

*I am sleeping. In my dream there is a baby—
a very small baby—holding on to my leg and
crying. She seems to be begging me to save her.
I do not know what to do. I look at her, and I feel
completely helpless. The baby slumps to the ground,
dead. I close my eyes in despair. When I open them, the
Mahanta is standing in front of me, gazing deeply into
my eyes. I look at the Master and back at the baby girl.
I still don't know what to do, so I walk away.*

* * *

Suddenly I was awakened from this dream by my
wife's screams. Only six months pregnant, she seemed
to be in labor. It was too early for the baby to come.
I began to sing HU, the beautiful love song to God, to
relax my fears, coaxing my wife to join me. As we sang
together, she quieted, and suddenly I slipped back into
the dream I had just awakened from.

* * *

*Once more, the baby girl is crying and holding on
to my leg. I know I am somehow supposed to help her.
I pick her up and hand her to the Master, who is once
again standing in front of me. The Master smiles and*

105

gives the ancient blessing of the Vairagi Masters, "May the blessings be."

* * *

When I returned to ordinary consciousness, I reassured my wife. "Don't worry. The Master is taking over everything. You will be OK." Her pain abated, and comforted, she fell asleep. When she awoke the following morning she was fine. The contractions had stopped, and she had no more problems with the pregnancy.

Three months later, when my wife was to give birth, I went with her to the hospital. While she was in labor, I waited alone in a mosquito-infested waiting room. I could hear my wife in the delivery room chanting the spiritual name of the Living ECK Master, "Wah Z, Wah Z, Wah Z," over and over again, the sound blending with the buzzing of the mosquitoes in the waiting room.

To take my mind off the mosquitoes and my wife's pain, I sang HU. Around two o'clock in the morning I fell into another vivid dream.

* * *

I see my wife delivering our baby girl. Right then my aunt sends me home to get something for her. When I get there, I can't find what she wants. As I am searching, I accidentally tip a lantern over, sending burning kerosene flowing toward my wife and our newborn daughter. I hasten to put out the fire, and my family is safe.

* * *

Twelve hours after I awoke from this dream, my baby daughter arrived in the world. I was so happy to meet her at last, but I still wondered about the three inner experiences I had had.

The night after I brought my wife and baby home from the hospital, they were asleep in the bedroom while I slept on the couch. Around two o'clock in the morning, the same time as my dream in the hospital waiting room, I woke up and went into the bedroom to check on them. My wife had left a candle burning on the table so the room would have light if she needed to attend to the baby. The candle had fallen over and was beginning to burn the carpet in the room. I woke my wife, and we quickly ran for water to put the fire out.

"Can you see the Master's hand in this?" I asked my wife. "Can you see how the Master is with us? Twice, while singing HU, we have experienced the protection of the Master for this child, first when you started labor too early and now to save you both from being burned."

Every day I look at my wife and my child and myself—and I understand the loving protection of the Master. We give thanks together to the Mahanta for this great gift of life.

25

Finding a Dream Job

Ami Bourne-Nisson

One Thursday in the middle of November, I lost my job. Just three months before, I'd left a secure position for this one, sure it was my next career step.

Now it was gone. Poof! But why? I'd done my best. My boss had raved about me constantly to the placement agency.

Monday morning the agency offered me a temporary assignment stuffing envelopes and sorting papers until a new position was found for me. It wasn't engaging work, but it was better than nothing. After a week the manager came to me.

"Would you like to interview for this job?" she asked. "The woman we hired is not going to take it after all."

Surprised, I thought about her offer. The people here were certainly friendly, and I seemed to fit right in. Was a boring job better than no job at all? I silently sang HU, the ancient name for God, as I considered what to say.

I flashed back to my first thought upon hearing of my dismissal from the previous job: *Perhaps this seeming failure is an opportunity.* I would love to adjust my work schedule to allow time for my first love, writing.

One of my manuscripts had been a recent finalist in a New York publisher's contest. So I knew my writing held potential.

All this went through my mind in a matter of moments, as the manager awaited an answer. I shook my head. "No, but thank you," I heard myself say. "I think I need something more challenging."

Two weeks passed. My husband, Burdoc, and I did a lot of talking and figuring. Even if I worked two part-time jobs, we couldn't make ends meet. I kept scanning the want ads and contemplating what to do. Meanwhile, the temporary job stretched on.

On Friday of my third week my fourteen-year-old son called. "There's a message for Papa on the answering machine," he told me.

"Oh? What's it about?"

"Some man wants to know if Papa's still interested in a programming job."

My heart skipped a beat. Wow! When had Burdoc applied for a new job? "Call Papa right away and give him the message," I told my son. "He'll have to call this man quickly or wait until Monday."

Burdoc didn't reach his caller. That night I had a dream: Burdoc and I were working with a camera crew, scouting an appropriate place to film. We all walked up a great grassy hill studded with bright flowers. The cameraman decided this was indeed the right place to film, but it was getting dark. I tried to turn on some light with a remote control, but it still wasn't bright enough. We'd found the right place but would simply have to wait for the dawn.

I wrote the dream in my journal and considered its meaning. Everything was set and ready to go; we just had to wait for the proper time.

Monday evening Burdoc managed to reach the man

about the job. They scheduled an interview for Thursday, four weeks to the day after I'd lost my job. Burdoc said the interview was intense. Over a late dinner, he smiled and asked me, "Do you remember why we decided to come to West Lafayette?"

I nodded. After two years of teaching in the United Arab Emirates, my husband had decided to follow his dream: to design computer software. He especially loved the idea of designing artificial-intelligence programs. We thought he'd need more schooling to break into that specific job market, so we moved near Purdue University.

"This company designs software," he told me, eyes aglow. "They have their own line of products and develop specific applications for their customers. And," he added significantly, "they are working on building artificial-intelligence programs."

I laughed. Not only would his dream job provide substantially more pay, but the corporate headquarters was less than five minutes from the house we'd just bought.

It looked perfect, but would it really happen?

That night I awoke around 2:00 a.m. to find Burdoc staring at the ceiling, "Can't sleep?" I asked.

"I just had the most amazing dream," he said.

"Can you tell me about it?"

He rose on his elbow. "It was so real. I was standing in front of the office building where I interviewed tonight. It wasn't quite the same, but I knew it was that place.

"In the dream, the building was situated beside a cove. We were all standing out at the water's edge, and everyone was very excited because my ships were coming in."

"Your ships?" I repeated foggily.

"Yes. The sun was shining, the water was clear, and here came these two ships."

"No wonder you couldn't sleep."

"The symbol is obvious, isn't it? My ships coming in. They were very big and bright with flat, glass bottoms so they could maneuver in shallow waters, and they were tied together."

"Tied together?"

"Yes, with cables. They were situated so the ships could travel side by side without encumbering each other."

"Kind of like us, huh?"

He looked at me in puzzlement.

"The way we are in our marriage. Tied together but not fettered."

He smiled. "Yes. Like that."

"When your ship comes in, mine will too," I concluded with satisfaction.

A lot of energy built up around us during the weekend. The first in a series of odd mechanical mishaps occurred Saturday morning, when Burdoc and I went to the bank machine to get some cash. The machine took our card and returned a receipt, but didn't give us any money. Not a major problem, but quite a nuisance to get to the bank on a busy Saturday morning to straighten the situation out.

On Tuesday morning Burdoc left for work in the car as usual. But when he stepped on the brakes, nothing happened! He just managed to avoid rear-ending our children's school bus.

Burdoc came back to the house, and we strategized on how to get through the coming days. "Keep singing HU," we reminded each other as we parted for the day. The song of HU was the best way to keep things in balance while navigating the highly charged energy fields around us.

That evening I interviewed for a part-time job and was hired on the spot.

Thursday when I turned on our oven, it abruptly died. Things were haywire everywhere. We reminded each other to keep singing HU!

A week had passed since Burdoc's interview. We were due to hear the verdict any day by mail. With Burdoc at this new job, I daydreamed, I could work part-time and write.

Again, it was my fourteen-year-old son who made the crucial call, as I was finishing my last day at the temporary job.

"It's here," he shouted. I gave him special permission to open the letter and read it. The offer was everything we had hoped for! I thanked my son and called Burdoc with the glad news.

Our ships had indeed come in. They rode on the heels of what the world might see as failure. I call it the miraculous workings of the Mahanta and the ECK!

26

The Tools of Mastery

David Purnell

I have a friend I'll call Gordon, who shares a house with his father. Gordon was experiencing intense spiritual distress. Nothing in his life seemed to be going right.

It came to a head one night while Gordon was driving home.

His car began making dreadful sounds. When he got home, he went to the garage to look for some tools in his father's toolbox. But the garage light wasn't working. With the dim light coming from the kitchen, Gordon found the garage lightbulb and replaced it with a new one. Clicking the switch again, there still was no light.

It was late, and he didn't want to wake his father. But Gordon had an important meeting the next day and needed to fix the car before morning. As gently as he could, Gordon woke his father and asked if he knew where there was a flashlight so he could look for the toolbox.

Groggily, the older man replied that there were some big flashlights on a top shelf in the garage. But to reach the shelf Gordon would have to get out the ladder. His father said there was also a small penlight flashlight in the bottom kitchen-cabinet drawer. But he cautioned Gordon that it wouldn't provide much light. He suggested that the larger flashlights would work much better.

In the kitchen, Gordon stopped at the cabinet drawer. He wasn't in the mood to haul out the ladder to climb up to find the big flashlights. He just wanted to find the toolbox so he could check his car. So he opened the kitchen drawer and, after a minute of rummaging, found the flashlight crammed among assorted gadgets and gizmos.

It didn't offer much light, but Gordon decided he could get by with it.

In the garage, he spent the next hour fumbling in the dark, struggling with the little flashlight. Pointing the tiny cone of light, he could see an area of only about five inches in diameter at a time. He thought he knew the garage, but in the darkness it seemed as though he was stumbling through the back of some strange theater.

He knocked over a tin of nails, tacks, and screws that scattered across the concrete floor. He hit his head several times on pipes and boards that were jutting out. Still, he was determined and dedicated to get by with what he had. Finally he stepped on an upturned tack. It punctured his shoe and pierced his foot. Teetering off balance, he crashed into a pan of what he later found was transmission fluid. The slippery oil oozed along the floor beneath his foot. Arms flailing, he annihilated an army of unseen objects that were dozing on tables and shelves. The concrete floor came up fast, and it was merciless.

Bruised and scraped, Gordon made a few more feeble attempts to find the errant toolbox. Finally, he had had enough and decided to call it a night.

Gordon's final thoughts before dropping off to sleep

were directed to his inner spiritual guide: *What is the waking dream here? Mahanta, what are you trying to tell me?*

The next morning, seated at the breakfast table with his father, Gordon bemoaned his late-night fiasco and failure to find the toolbox. "First of all," his father said, "you could have saved yourself a lot of aggravation if you had just taken the time to find the ladder and get the big flashlights."

After a pause, he added, "When was the time last time you opened your trunk? Don't you remember that we put the toolbox in the back of your car about three months ago? You've been driving around with it all this time."

After this, Gordon took a long hard look at what the Mahanta was trying to show him through the waking dream that night.

The first connection he made was that he had been skimping on the Spiritual Exercises of ECK for a long time. He realized the ladder was a symbol for the spiritual exercises. The ladder would make it possible to reach the bigger flashlights—allowing him to see what he needed to see. Allowing more light into his world.

The final realization was that he already had the tools to make the needed repairs—on his car and in his life. A little more light makes all the difference!

I recognized this as the Golden-tongued Wisdom—
a message that appears in our daily life to give us
spiritual reassurance. I knew I was on the right track.

27

License-Plate Wisdom

Adele Jones

*M*y husband and I have three grown children, two girls and a boy. Each has been diagnosed as psychotic. A year before our son was diagnosed, I had a disturbing dream. I saw our two daughters in a very old asylum. As I watched, the door opened, and in came two vicious-looking nurses, carrying our son in restraints. My heart fell.

When I awoke, I wrote the dream in my journal, adding a note at the end: "This has happened in the dream state. It need not happen in the physical."

But it did happen in the physical. I could hardly bear the pain of my son's illness. I kept asking the Mahanta, my inner teacher, "Please show me. What do I need to learn from this tragedy? If I have made mistakes, please show me how to get it right this time."

One day I received a phone call from our son's neighbor. She asked me to come right away. My son would need to be taken to the hospital. During the three-hour drive, I sang HU, the ancient love song to God, watching for signs that the Mahanta was with me. In the very beauty of the day I felt he knew and understood my concern.

Knowing it would be very difficult to persuade my son to go to the hospital, I arranged for the supervising

nurse to come and help me. My son was suicidal. The
nurse gave him the choice of going willingly with me
or being committed by a court. He chose to go with me.

It was a dreadful drive to the hospital. My son
banged his feet on the floor and his fists on the dash-
board, and attempted several times to unfasten his
seat belt so he could jump out of the car. "Why are you
doing this to me? I've done nothing to deserve this
treatment. Take me home!" he yelled.

I quietly sang HU and kept driving, inwardly asking for understanding.

The first help appeared on a license plate: *KARMA*.
I recognized this as the Golden-tongued Wisdom—a
message that appears in our daily life to give us spiritual reassurance. I knew I was on the right track. I
tucked that piece of understanding away and continued on to the hospital.

I stopped at the front door and released my son into
the care of a nurse. Then I drove to the parking lot,
where I found a second bit of Golden-tongued Wisdom.
I parked beside a yellow car with the license plate *HU*.

Later, while I was waiting for the doctor to examine
and admit my son, I went for a walk. There, parked
on the street, was a blue van with gold lettering on the
side: *DUNN WELL DRIVING SCHOOL!* My third
confirmation.

I realized that I had done what was karmically
necessary for my children and for myself. The meaning
of the many dream experiences I had had with our
children over the years became clearer. The ECK, Divine
Spirit, knew what was right for us all. Through my
pain, I have learned to accept their illness and allow
them to live with it as best they can.

On this journey, the Golden-tongued Wisdom had
told me I had it right this time.

28

Navigating a Turning Point

Laurence Cruz

*F*or a decade, I dreamed of moving from my home in England to the United States—a country I felt more in tune with than any other. I had even tried to make the move once, but it hadn't worked out. Then, four years ago, I felt the window opening again, but the details—the when and where—were still unclear.

Sri Harold Klemp, the Mahanta, the Living ECK Master, once described a turning point as life's way of helping us move ahead spiritually. But, he added, we must reach for the gift ourselves.

I had been reaching for years. I had scouted numerous areas of the United States on previous visits, trying to find which area suited me best. Now I had applications pending for three different courses of study in two different cities—Los Angeles and Seattle—to help me combine a career change with my move. I had saved some money and paid all my debts.

I was ready.

Despite all this, I still wanted some confirmation that the move I was planning was in my best spiritual interest. It was not without its risks. I had no permanent visa or job offer waiting for me in America. But I was more comfortable in the U.S. than I had ever been in London. Even though I had family there, and my professional life was blossoming into exciting new—and lucrative—areas. Was it really a good time to be gallivanting off to a new and uncertain life on another continent?

By August I had become nearly desperate for answers. I wrote in my journal every day. As soon as I got home from work, I would sit down for a long, deep spiritual exercise, hoping to find some confirmation of my plans. Finally, one day after attending an ECK seminar, my inner guide parted the veil.

That morning I woke with a sore throat. I was a teacher and needed to be able to project my voice. I decided to call in sick so the school could arrange for a substitute teacher. Half asleep, I reached from my bed for the textbook I used with my class, so I could tell the school which page we were studying. When I opened the book, my index finger was placed exactly under two words: "Destination: Seattle." The book was some two hundred pages long!

In Eckankar, we refer to a spiritually important insight that comes through written or spoken words in daily life as the Golden-tongued Wisdom. This was definitely that, but I still wasn't satisfied. I wanted more confirmation!

Two days later it came. Walking to a meeting in central London, I passed an open-air restaurant from which a radio was blaring. At the very moment I walked by, the radio announcer's voice boomed, "It is indeed Seattle!"

The clincher came a few nights later. Of the three courses I had applied for, only one—a nine-month screen-writing class in Seattle—worked out. And of the three, it was the class that had really made my heart sing. As a finishing touch, the class was scheduled to begin on October 22—the start of the ECK Spiritual New Year.

Since my move to Seattle, I have earned a master's degree and completed my career change, and my employer has sponsored me to remain in the United States.

To be sure, my new life in America is rich with fresh challenges, but I'm better equipped to deal with them after navigating this turning point.

Doing so required courage, resourcefulness, imagination, judgment, patience, careful planning, hard work, and spiritual initiative. But most of all, it required trust in Divine Spirit and an open and loving heart. In return, Spirit placed one stepping-stone after another in front of my faltering steps until I arrived at my goal.

29

The Spiritual Garbage Collector

Peter Plumb

*L*ately I had felt fearful about my spiritual growth and some of the problems I had been wrestling with. One beautiful morning, to get my attention off my troubles, I headed to the mall with my friend Paul to visit an art museum. On our way, we decided to take advantage of the glorious day by sitting on a bench in a quiet corner of the mall park to do a spiritual exercise.

We began to sing HU, the beautiful and ancient name for God, moving deeper and deeper into contemplation as we sang. Suddenly, Paul nudged me. "Look at this," he whispered.

I opened my eyes just in time to see a gigantic garbage truck pull up practically on my foot.

"Pusssh!" The truck let out a loud air-brake sound. I almost jumped over the back of the bench!

I looked up to see the driver chuckling at me and shaking his head. The crew picked up the garbage, and off they went.

Paul and I looked at each other and asked, "What's *that* waking dream all about?" It didn't take long to figure out what the Mahanta was trying to show me through this unusual event: If you do your spiritual exercises faithfully, you will get rid of your garbage. But don't be startled when the Mahanta, the inner teacher, arrives to take it away.

I had to laugh at Divine Spirit's sense of humor. Now I could relax and let the "spiritual garbage collector" do his work.

30

The Cry of the Hawk

Bonnie Anderson

*M*y husband and I had just set out on a road trip to Milwaukee, Wisconsin. As we cruised along, memories of childhood family trips ran pleasantly through my mind.

A hawk circling above the highway caught my eye. Hadn't I just read an article by my spiritual teacher, Sri Harold Klemp? Something about the "cry of the hawk?" What was that about? I made a mental note to look it up when I got home.

A few miles later we approached a railway overpass. A boxcar parked on the tracks bore the words *Milwaukee Road* in faded paint. I went on alert. Two waking dreams—distinct messages for me—in a few minutes, and we hadn't even left the Twin Cities metro area yet!

Being on the road felt so good. It set my mind to wandering lightly over the attraction to Native American life I have felt since I was a tiny child.

"Did I mention my family had one of the first pop-up tent trailers manufactured?" I asked my husband. At that very moment a tent trailer pulled ahead of us in the left lane. "Apache," I said. "That was the name of the tent trailer we traveled with!"

As the car and trailer passed, it was like something

had shifted inside of me. Certain puzzle pieces fell into place and made sense. I suddenly knew the reason for this road trip and the answer to a certain yearning that had started when I was only two years old.

My family had taken a vacation in the Black Hills of South Dakota. There we met a tribal chief who liked to visit and talk with the tourists. Normally fearful of strangers, I immediately reached out to this chief adorned with moccasins, beaded neck- and armbands, leather loincloth, and eagle feathers in his hair. My mother had told me this story many times over the years.

Two or three years later, at our summer camp on Thornapple Lake in Michigan, we attended a tribal festival and pow-wow in a park. I was entranced with a ceremony in which the tribe adopted an entire white family.

I wanted to be adopted by the tribe too and go live with them. When the ceremony concluded and it was time to return to our campground across the lake, we got in our small blue fishing boat with a ten-horse outboard engine for the short trip. The pow-wow was over. But not for me.

I successfully pestered my family to let me go back to visit the park with my teenage sister, Anne. We returned across the lake in our little boat. Anne found the chief and explained what I wanted.

The old man smiled kindly down at me and spoke a word in his own tongue. "All you have to do is say this word and you will be adopted by the tribe," he said.

At four or five, the word was incomprehensible to me. My mouth couldn't form it. Time stood still as I stood mute before the chief. I simply couldn't speak.

My sister and I headed back across the lake in our little blue boat. As young as I was, I realized something:

I was exactly where I was meant to be in this lifetime. I was in the family I belonged with. It was a timeless moment of Soul-awareness.

The Apache tent trailer was fading in the distance, far ahead of my husband and me. As I watched it go, I realized a long-sought connection between my past and present.

The tent trailer of today resembled the Plains Indian travois used to pull tents and gear in the past. I had been given glimmers of the lifetime my family and I had most certainly shared in that environment. As we traveled across the country in the 1950s and 60s, we visited many national parks and wilderness areas. Dad exuded a reverence for all life that was most at home in the great outdoors, and he shared this legacy with us all.

Back home after our weekend in Milwaukee, I remembered to look up the article by Sri Harold Klemp. "According to Native American legend," he had written, "the hawk's cry—a shrill whistle—is to pierce the awareness and awaken people to a state of full awareness. . . . So the symbol of the hawk is about having a clear spiritual vision."

Long before our weekend journey, the Mahanta had confirmed my revelations and remembrances along Milwaukee Road.

31

Working the Waking Dream

Robert Claycomb

ome years ago, I was considering a course in speed-reading and approached a teacher whose opinions I respected for advice. "Does this technique work?" I asked.

"You have to work *it*," he replied firmly.

Although I never took the course, I applied his sound advice to a different technique: paying attention to guidance from the Holy Spirit, which often comes through waking dreams.

Waking dreams are unusual coincidences or symbols that crop up in your daily life to answer spiritual questions. Sometimes if you have a specific dilemma, you can set up your own, easy-to-understand symbol and what it will mean when you see it.

Last fall, I was contemplating finding a new job. Possibilities for further promotions or raises seemed slim at my firm.

Then two interesting positions were posted in the company cafeteria. Each was a grade higher in pay and responsibilities than my current job. This was such a rare occurrence that I had to follow up.

As I hurried to the personnel office my mind was spinning. Was this really the right thing to do? Should I leave a job I liked for the unknown? Would I spend a year or two adapting and learning new things, only to find I didn't like it? Would I leave my department in the lurch?

Since it was Friday, I decided to ponder my application over the weekend.

That night I sat silently in contemplation and asked the Mahanta, my spiritual guide, for a waking dream. I needed a clear sign to proceed with this job hunt or stay put. My first thought was to use red and green traffic lights as a waking-dream symbol for myself— red for no, green for yes—but they are too common. I would get even more confused. Suddenly a dream I once had of an elephant popped in my head.

Red and green elephants! That would really be a good test. If I saw a red elephant, I would stop looking for a new job. A green elephant would confirm my application.

I implored the ECK, Holy Spirit, to send this unusual symbol in a dream, a cartoon on TV, a billboard, or anywhere It saw fit. Then I would have a sure answer.

I awoke the next morning and recorded my dreams. No elephants had shown up. To engage my mind fully in the issue at hand, I filled out the application forms from work and updated my résumé. I tried to keep my mind off the waking dream, but by midmorning Sunday, with still no elephants in sight, I thought, *I'll go to work and print a nice laser copy of the résumé. That way, if the elephant is green, I'll be ready.*

In the office I turned on a computer, popped in my disk, and tried to open the file. But the screen fluttered and the program crashed. Did my disk have the wrong format? I persisted until I found a machine that opened my file. But when I tried to print it, the text came out skewed and distorted.

This is nuts, I said to myself. Before giving up I went

upstairs to the computer in my lab to try one last time.

As I sat in front of the computer, my eyes came to rest on the desk before me. There beside the telephone was my answer.

My supervisor had recently hired a postdoctoral fellow from India to work in the lab. As is the tradition in his country, he'd brought a gift for his new employer. It was a hand-sized elephant sculpted in red clay.

"There it is," I whispered as a smile crept across my face. I put my résumé away and went home. I felt relieved to know I had followed my waking dream. I realized I was really very happy with my job. Sometimes revelations turn out to reflect what the heart has known all along.

What I didn't know was that there was more to come.

Three weeks later, a notice came from the administrator's office. Research positions were being rescaled and everyone at my level would advance a grade. Pay increases would be retroactive for a month. I got the promotion and the raise after all!

This adventure is only one example of how waking dreams work. It is one fun way Eckankar has helped me participate more fully in the mystery of life. Try it for yourself—but remember, you have to really pay attention and work it!

32

"You Are Cured"

Hallie Shepherd

The year was 1982, right after my thirty-first birthday. My thirteen-year-old niece, Becky, had just come home from school with some great news. She'd won first place in an art contest and was headed to Texas for a national art show.

I got so excited I chased her around the front lawn. We were like two puppies frolicking on a warm spring day, romping and rolling in the grass.

All of a sudden, I felt completely drained of energy. My muscles felt like those of a newborn babe. I was almost too weak to sit up. I felt zapped of all energy and strength. *Gee,* I thought, *maybe I'm coming down with a horrible case of the flu.*

That night we were going to take Becky out to dinner to celebrate her good news. So rather than let the illness take hold, I dragged myself into the bathroom. A nice, long, relaxing soak in the tub was my cure for stress and illness. I felt lightheaded as I lay there soaking. But I was determined to outrun this illness.

This strategy usually works for me, but it didn't this time. As I attempted to get out of the tub, I almost passed out. Every time I tried to crawl out, I got dizzy. Lights danced in front of my eyes, and I almost fainted.

I collapsed back in the bathtub and finally found

the strength to pound on the wall and call for help. Paramedics and the fire department were quickly summoned. When the paramedics took my vital signs, they found I had almost no blood pressure. I was pretty close to death.

I spent a week in the hospital, while every conceivable test was run. I had CAT scans, I was poked and prodded, and the doctors took what seemed like pints of blood. I saw doctor after doctor; each tried to figure out what was making me so weak.

Finally they sent me home. The next day, my primary doctor called me. "Hallie," he said, "I'm afraid I have some bad news. You have a very rare condition called Addison's disease."

"What's that?" I asked.

"Addison's disease is a complete shutdown of your adrenal glands. It's rare and used to be fatal," he said. "Now it can be controlled by medications, usually some form of steroid." He then said I'd have to take cortisone every day of my life.

Needless to say, with such a strong remedy, I needed careful monitoring. The best doctors were a few hours away in San Francisco. So for three years, I faithfully traveled into the city every six months for careful monitoring by an endocrinologist.

I usually stayed at my brother Phil's house in Marin County, which is close to San Francisco. Phil was a member of Eckankar. I had also become a member in the 1970s but I had later dropped away.

I was familiar with the ideas of Eckankar, and Phil kept me posted on new developments. I looked forward to seeing him each time I went to San Francisco. We would visit, and then I would sleep in the guest room. On one visit, the night before my appointment, I had a very vivid dream.

In the dream, the Mahanta, the Living ECK Master came to me. He bathed me in the most beautiful, radiant white light. It was like being wrapped in the warmest, softest cotton I could imagine.

Love and warmth gently showered down on me. Then the Mahanta whispered the words, "You are cured."

With startling clarity, I saw all my bodies—mental, causal, emotional, and physical—begin to shimmer and vibrate with white light. It looked like white soda pop bubbling and flowing through me. My bodies became perfectly aligned and in harmony with life.

Later that day I hurried to my appointment. When the doctor came in the room, I blurted out, "I don't think I have Addison's disease anymore."

He looked at me very skeptically. "What makes you say that? You must remember that only about twenty-eight cases in medical history have ever been reversed."

Now what was I supposed to tell this man of science? "Gee, Doc, I have this spiritual guide, and in a dream he said I was cured."

I didn't think that was the approach to take. So rather than explaining, I just asked the doctor to test me again. He grudgingly obliged.

I'll never forget the look on his face when he got the results of those tests. He went back over every test I had ever taken, to make sure I'd really had Addison's disease to begin with. Then he looked at me with a quizzical expression. "You are indeed cured," he announced. "We better start tapering you off that medication."

This gift of love from the Mahanta brought me back to Eckankar. It showed me that once you have accepted the Living ECK Master as your guide, you will always be under his umbrella of love and protection. As the Wayshower, he gives us the opportunity to resolve karma and work through the most difficult problems.

The Shariyat-Ki-Sugmad, Book One, (part of the scriptures of ECK) points out that the Mahanta does not perform miracles merely because we ask him to. I learned that the Mahanta gave me a gift of love because it was time for me to move forward on my journey home to God. I am so grateful!

I was describing the type of vehicle that brought me the message when a lightbulb went on. It came from my dear friend, the Mahanta, always by my side!

33

A Simple Technique to Get Answers to Any Question

Michael Bell

*T*he presence of my inner guide, the Mahanta, has been constantly with me since I became a member of Eckankar. His unique signature is a blue, six-pointed star or a blue globe of light you glimpse out of the corner of your eye.

Over the years, important decisions in my life have often presented themselves with several possible solutions. It's not that I can't think what to do—it's that all solutions seem acceptable. How can I judge which is best for my highest spiritual goals?

At this point I turn it over to the Mahanta. Many times I ask for answers via a waking dream. This is a coincidence or symbol in your everyday life that catches your attention and seems to speak directly to your problem.

Recently I started a small business managing apartments in my spare time. Soon it developed into a full-time career.

The snag was that I already had a job as a military pilot. In fact I was only a couple of years away from retirement. My days were busy flying, and my nights were overflowing as I managed the rental properties. I was about to crack from exhaustion and stress.

My choices included selling the properties, hiring a manager, or not flying. Which would be best for my spiritual growth? And a fourth choice hovered at the edge of my consciousness: maybe I could keep the properties and become a guard bum.

"Guard bum" is a slang term for a part-time National Guard pilot. As a guard bum I wouldn't get immediate retirement, but eventually it would come.

The harder I thought about it, the less I knew what to do. For weeks it haunted me. I took it into contemplation and watched my dreams and waking state. "Please, Mahanta, give me some clue," I pleaded. Then my answer came.

I was driving home after a long day of flying, once again trying to sort out the dilemma. A car careened across three lanes to cut right in front of me.

I strained to read its license plate. It read "Be a Bum 3"! My jaw dropped in disbelief as the car left via the next exit ramp.

Could it really be that simple? I was overjoyed, but giving up a full immediate military pension wasn't easy.

I knew it was the answer, but I wanted to validate it. That night I wrote the incident in my journal. I was describing the type of vehicle that brought me the message when a lightbulb went on. It came from my old friend, the Mahanta, always by my side!

How did I know? I looked down at the words: "The car was a blue Escort."

This is how the Mahanta escorts me through all my trials. I'm much happier flying with the National Guard and managing my rental properties, with time to enjoy life and relax at least once a week.

34

Healing of a Mother's Heart

Helga Hoffmann

In 1991 my husband and I lost our only child, our daughter. She died in a car accident at age twenty-one. She was buried in Germany in the town where I was born, so when we visited my father several times a year we always visited her grave nearby.

Visiting my daughter's grave was always a very painful experience for me. At the cemetery, I often felt so overcome by grief and pain that it almost choked me. I wondered if I would ever be healed of this intense pain. Then an unexpected gift of healing came.

Two years ago, we were preparing to visit my father. Before the trip I had two strong dreams. In the first one, my husband and I were in a cemetery—little more than a field of weeds near a street. We were looking for a grave site, but we couldn't find it. In the second dream I asked my father, "Where's Hilde?" Hilde is my stepmother.

He said, "Oh, she's out working."

In the dream I said, "I'll go to the cemetery by myself then." But my father said, "The cemetery isn't there anymore."

In the dream I insisted on going. My father came with me, so I wouldn't be alone. When we got there, all the graves and flowers were gone. Instead there were weeds, stones, and parched earth—a terrible place, like a desert.

My father said, "See, I told you. You shouldn't have come."

A few days after I had these two unusual dreams, we arrived in Germany. My husband and I went to the cemetery to visit my daughter's grave, and again I was overcome with pain.

That night, after I did my spiritual exercise, the Blue Light came. I knew this special light was a sign of the Mahanta. I don't know if I fell asleep or if I was still awake, but the light was fluid and shone all over me. I was wrapped in it. A wind blew very strongly and caressed my face, while the light shone over me in different shades of blue.

In the morning when I woke up, I knew something in my heart had changed. When we went back to the cemetery that afternoon and I stood by my daughter's grave, there was no more pain, no more sadness. It was all gone.

Then I understood what the two dreams meant. My daughter isn't there at the grave site; it is only a piece of barren land. A wonderful sense of healing came over me with the understanding that we don't ever lose our loved ones. They are always with us as Soul.

35

My Job or My Life?

Russell Torlage

One day at work, my manager approached me. Because I had strong computer skills, I was asked to consider heading up a special project. Although my expertise did not cover all the project requirements, I accepted. The job turned out to be very demanding.

After a year and a half, I took a mental inventory of the assignment. The stress of the position was having a heavy impact on my personal life. I wasn't practicing my spiritual exercises regularly. Even though that twenty minutes a day of quiet contemplation was vital to my spiritual health, my attitude now was just to get them over with. I was eating poorly and sleeping poorly. Many of my fun projects had been put on hold indefinitely.

I wanted out of the assignment, but I felt guilty about abandoning the project. I also worried about jeopardizing my chances for any future job promotions. *But what's more important, my job or my life?* I asked myself. After three days of mental acrobatics, I still could not decide what to do. I needed help from the ECK, the Holy Spirit.

One night before nodding off for the evening, I asked the Mahanta, my spiritual guide, to show me the answer in a dream. I promised to act on the dream no matter what the message.

That night I dreamed I was driving down a road in a car I had recently sold. Although snow covered the ground, the car's windows were down. It was almost dark. Up ahead a deer was grazing on the road. Seeing this gentle creature brought joy to my heart. Then I caught a glimpse of two pairs of shining eyes in the dark beyond the deer—two wolves. One made a large circle around the deer. It joined the other wolf, and I could see them planning their attack. Then to my horror both wolves charged the deer and ripped it to pieces.

Shocked at what was unfolding in front of me, I feared for my own safety. I managed to roll the windows up. I wanted desperately to accelerate past the wolves while they were attacking the deer, but my tires spun in the snow. I eased my foot off the accelerator, and finally the wheels gained traction. The wolves didn't notice me. They carried the deer carcass in front of the car and off to the left.

As I motored away, I saw one of the foremen from work walking toward me on the left. He looked confused as I drove past him because of the car I was in and the direction I was going.

When I woke up, I analyzed my dream. My old car represented the job position I held before taking on my new assignment. The deer represented my previous peaceful state of consciousness. The first wolf that scouted out its prey was my immediate boss. The second wolf was my boss's boss. Both of them were involved in the decision to approach me about the new assignment.

The killing of the deer showed me the destruction of my personal life. To my managers, the corporation's appetite was all that mattered. My career was unimportant. Later I would find out that there was no future in my new position after all.

Driving past the wolves indicated that my fate would change. The fact that the two wolves were more interested in the carcass than in me showed me that my best interests were not being served. The responsibility to live my life as I deemed fit would be mine and mine alone. Passing my coworker showed me that my peers would be very surprised at my decision to return to my old position.

This dream showed me that if I quit the project, my life would continue in a better direction where I could again find balance in all areas, especially my spiritual life.

First thing the next morning I made an appointment to meet with my boss. I was nervous, but I knew what I had to do. The ECK had showed me in no uncertain terms. It was up to me to trust in the Mahanta, to stand up and take charge of my life and my future. Two and a half hours later I had resigned.

Since then my life has certainly changed for the better. I have more time to devote to my ECK responsibilities. I enrolled in an engineering course that time restrictions and pressure had prevented me from taking. I was able to complete all of the little projects that had been on hold, and start many other new projects.

This dream was a gift of awareness. It brought a deeper insight into my life and showed me that the creative power of Divine Spirit is in each and every one of us. Most important, it convinced me that the Mahanta always has my best interests at heart.

36

I Was Healed in My Dream

Marrian Kangenya

Ten years before I found Eckankar, I was always sick. My suffering took me to many hospitals and herbalists, but my search was in vain. I was unhappy, lonely, and dejected. Friends and some relatives avoided me. In spite of my prayers, my health deteriorated so much that it became difficult to talk. This increased my solitude even further.

Once when I was very ill, I went to sleep and dreamed. The dream stopped when I woke to go to work. The next night the dream continued where it had left off. The dream went on for three nights. This is the story that unfolded.

In my dream I woke to find myself walking along a white street. A voice called my name. Without hesitation I followed the voice. It came from a distant place which resolved into a huge white hall. As I walked toward the hall, a big door opened for me. Inside the building, three men were seated around a big beautiful table. A light too brilliant for my eyes sat on the table. I approached the men and stood with my head bowed.

The first man bowed in greeting and spoke. "Welcome, my child. You are starting your journey now. It's up to you whether you accomplish it or not.

"Your meandering road is painted white. It travels

across rivers and oceans and will lead you to a small, white house."

The second man said, "When you reach the house, say this word, then knock on the door, and it will open." He said a word.

The third man pointed to my right to show me that a horse laden with blankets, water, and food waited for me. Nearby a man and his horse stood motionless, ready to accompany me on my long journey. Without knowing how it happened, I was already on horseback. My journey had started.

The horseman never spoke a word. He knew when I wanted water or food. Our journey took many years. I was weak and sick along the way.

Again without knowing how it happened, I found myself standing at the door of a bright, white house. My horse and companion disappeared into thin air. I stood alone. Fear swept over me, but then I remembered the word the second man in the hall had given me. I uttered the word and knocked. The door opened, and I entered.

The house was white inside as well. I looked down to see that a thick, white towel covered my entire body. Joy overwhelmed me as all my weakness faded away.

Two transparent beings with wings stood on either side of a bath filled with sparkling blue water. They asked me to step in. As I bathed, my attention was on their beautiful, snow-white wings. When I came out of the bath, they sprinkled my body with something from small containers they held. I was wrapped in a brilliant white towel. They directed me to a man seated at the far end of the building.

This great being was dressed in a maroon robe. On his head was a turban of white cloth. Drawn to this shining being, I bowed and knelt before him to hear what he had to say.

He raised his hand in blessing and said, "Go back into the world and finish your work." When I woke up, some of the pains had left my body. The healing process had begun.

Years later when I joined Eckankar, I recognized the great being who sent me back to earth as the ECK Master Fubbi Quantz, abbot of the Katsupari Monastery in northern Tibet. This Golden Wisdom Temple, located on a supraphysical level, is where I went in my dream for spiritual healing.

Since finding Eckankar, I now enjoy life fully. I walk in the Light and Sound of God every day of my life.

37

Sometimes the Key
Is Already in Your Hand

Melody Chang

*I*n 1998, I was happily studying in the United States. I had immersed myself in my studies to avoid facing the problems that awaited me back home in Asia. But my visa would expire at the end of the year. Somehow, I was going to have to return and face the situations—a broken marriage, financial problems, and a job I hated—that had made me so unhappy.

Three or more times a day, after hours of mental wrestling, I would arrive at decisions on how to solve these problems, only to have the solutions disintegrate before I could take action. I grew desperate as I contemplated my homecoming.

As a student of the teachings of Eckankar, I knew that dreams were important. But I didn't realize their power until three vivid dreams came that showed me my future and gave me the confidence to heal the past.

In the first dream, I was sitting in the passenger seat of an out-of-control car. There was no driver behind the wheel. I sat helplessly while the car hurtled onto a sidewalk and ran over a pedestrian. Oddly, the pedestrian was unhurt. He simply gazed at me with a look of casual curiosity.

In the dream I tried to stop the car but only succeeded in bending the steering wheel. Finally the car stopped on its own, and I sat there gasping and sweating with fear.

When I awoke, I realized my inner teacher, the Mahanta, was using the dream to show me something vital: even though it felt as if my life were out of control, I needed to rely on my inner guidance and let everything take its natural course. I had to let go of my fears and leave the driving to him.

This gave me courage to take the first step. I returned to Asia.

With constant attention to my inner guidance, I completed my divorce. Then I tackled my finances. I quit my job and set up my own company in hopes of putting an end to my financial difficulties once and for all. Each day I grew spiritually, overcoming my fears, and becoming more confident for my future, but my financial picture was still shaky. I had to make some decisions on how to improve my business. So I decided to sleep on it.

In the second vivid dream, I was playing cards with my friends and my father stood looking over my shoulder. I was dealt such a wonderful hand that I was able to win the game without even thinking. The dream seemed prophetic and left me feeling very hopeful.

It wasn't more than a few weeks later that I received an unexpected opportunity—contract work with a former employer. The good hand of cards I had been dealt in my dream had foretold this opportunity. The contract I had won without even thinking was a "good deal" which would be very profitable to my business.

The third dream of healing came not long after. I was climbing a high stone wall. I couldn't see the top, and about midway up I ran out of stepping-stones. The stone I stood on was so small that I had to cling tightly to two handholds above me to keep my balance. Exhausted, I was about to let go when I heard an inner message: *Sometimes the key is already in your hand.*

What does this mean? I wondered.

Following a nudge, I pushed lightly on the stone under my right palm. The wall rumbled, and the stones under my right hand toppled down, revealing a spacious resting place where I could regroup for my journey.

I feel very grateful to have had these three special dreams. Through them, I saw how the Mahanta was leading me from my troubles through the healing of my past, to a new confidence in my ability to handle problems with wisdom and composure. There is no doubt that the keys to our life are already in our hands.

Sometimes we just need a little time out—some time to dream our way to the next step on this spiritual journey called life.

38

Signs That Point
the Way Home

Tom Casad

*I*n 1994 my wife and I began to think about moving. Although we were happy in the Seattle area, a strong nudge to move had stayed with us for several months. Yet we did little more than research places to move to at the public library.

Finally my wife asked the Mahanta, our inner teacher, to confirm the move with a waking dream. Rather than just waiting to see what that sign might be, she declared that it would be four bald eagles flying in the same place. When she told me, I laughed. During our three years in Seattle, we had rarely seen even one eagle, let alone two. And more often than not, that eagle had been perched in a tree.

Not long after that, we were driving on a highway north of Seattle. Suddenly four bald eagles flew across our path. Then we saw two more, perhaps for emphasis.

Now we were faced with confirmation of what had only been an intuitive impression. Still, I balked. Any change is hard for me. So we asked the Mahanta to send another message. Something dramatic.

Nothing happened for a few months. Then one evening my wife and I were going out to dinner. Unusual for us, we were ready with half an hour to spare. With

157

time on our hands and the question of the move hanging over our heads, we decided to sit down in contemplation. We agreed to sing HU, our favorite sacred word, and ask the Mahanta if we really should move.

Ten minutes later we heard a knock at the front door. We decided to ignore it and closed our eyes again. Another knock came.

This time we answered the door to see our neighbor standing there. Did we smell smoke? We did. She said she was going to call the fire department, and we agreed she should. Confident the situation was under control, we returned to our spiritual exercise.

When it was time to leave for the restaurant, we discovered our car was blocked by a fire truck. The fire captain climbed down and asked us about the call they received. Then he walked around the building with us. He told us everything looked all right, got in the fire truck, and drove away.

I had forgotten about the question we had just posed to the Mahanta, but my wife had not. She eagerly asked if I had noticed the captain's name tag.

"It was Rideout!" she exclaimed.

This was enough confirmation. We decided to fulfill our obligations in town and move as soon as we could. It was the best decision we could have made. A year and a half later, we are happier than ever in our new home.

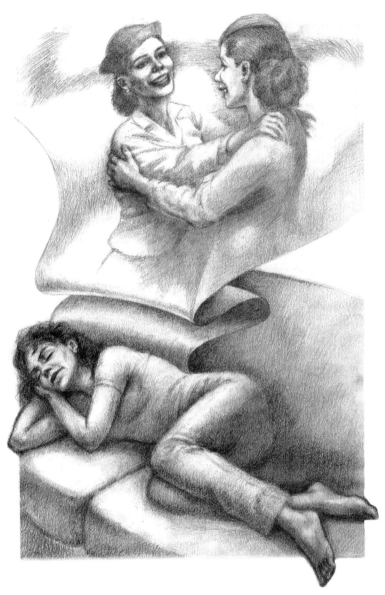

In her sister's embrace, my grandmother laughed
and looked as she had in her twenties. Here, I noticed,
she remembered who she really was.

39

Letting Go of a Loved One

Lynne Kieve

My grandmother was a favorite of many people. She was the person strangers approached for help on buses and trains, in restaurants and grocery stores. She always saw the best in people, and they were drawn to her warmth and told her their life stories.

She lived with us for a few years, before I started school, after my mother went back to work. Those years were the golden time of my childhood. With my grandmother, I had a true friend, a wealth of affection.

Every day she came into my room to admire the little designs I made with blocks and beads on top of my bedspread. We would marvel each morning at how we always ended up wearing the same color, as if we were made to be together, side by side. She had immeasurable patience with me at the piano, where we both agreed neither of us could sing; in the kitchen, where I was more work than help to her; and outdoors in the gardens, where we made up ridiculous stories until we collapsed in laughter. Those few years were precious and fleeting. I saw her once a year after that, but her love always surrounded me like a soft familiar shawl.

The last fifteen years of her life were challenging. She had several strokes and seizures that left her paralyzed and unable to speak. She often did not recognize me when I visited her, but I saw her regularly in my dreams.

Although outwardly she seemed to be in a world of her own, I knew that our special connection remained unbroken. I sensed that she was facing a part of her journey that did not include me.

About two months ago, I began to visit her in her nursing home on the inner planes during my contemplations and dreams. I helped her pack her belongings and knew she would soon leave her body behind and move on. The landscape through the nursing-home window was bright and sunny, with lush gardens, gently rolling hills, and blossoming trees teeming with the sound of birds. To me it seemed vibrant and pulsing with life. An exquisite light spilled into her room in this inner world, washing over the walls and bed. In these experiences, she was nervous about leaving, worried about what she perceived as failures in her life. But in my eyes, her struggles seemed so small compared to the extraordinary Soul I saw.

A few nights later, I dreamed of a graceful white swan, serene and peaceful. Its purity reminded me of a long-forgotten world I would someday rejoin. The next morning at work, I saw a photo of a white swan taped to the top of an office doorway.

That night, the Inner Master took me one more time to see my grandmother.

She had left her body the way one takes off a heavy, worn coat. I watched her greet her sister who had passed on over a year ago. In her sister's embrace, my grandmother laughed and looked as she had in her twenties. Here, I noticed, she remembered who she really was. They were so happy to see each other and the presence of God was so strong and sustaining that

I felt content to watch them walk off, arm in arm, with so much to talk about.

In the morning, my mother called long-distance to tell me my grandmother had passed on. She called again a few days later to tell me that my family was going to place my grandmother's ashes in the Hudson River at Cold Spring. From there, the river winds through the towns she visited as a child, to New York City where she grew up, and finally to the Atlantic Ocean, her most beloved place.

As she poured the ashes into the river, my mother told me that she whispered good-bye and said, "I will always love you." Then my mother looked up. Four white swans had gathered in the stillness of the water. They stayed there until my mother was ready to walk back to the car.

"She's with the swans now," my father said, as they drove away.

That morning, I sat on the edge of my bed to say good-bye to my grandmother. Faintly, I heard the sound of bagpipes filter into the room from far away. For an instant, I caught sight of her being carried into a vast ocean on a majestic clipper ship, its white sails unfurled. The sound coming from the ocean waves is beyond my ability to describe; all I know is that sound contains all that she loves, all that she is.

She is safe, I thought to myself, *and so dearly loved.* And because of this love, I know we will see each other when we need to. For now, I am still thanking her for passing on the torch of divine love.

40

How to Knock Down Fears

Larry White

*D*reams have helped me so many times that I can hardly recommend a better way of talking to God. A few years ago, fresh off the unemployment line, I was hired to abstract legal documents and information for a real-estate title insurance company. I had not been there long when my boss asked me to type the insurance policies.

Little did he know I couldn't type in the generally accepted way. I had my own method, which boiled down to every finger for itself. To show him I was eager for new responsibilities, I hit my keyboard so fast on that first day that even Bach would have been impressed. I was very proud until my boss began finding typographical errors. "Been to an eye doctor lately?" he asked, not totally ecstatic.

The next day I slowed down a little and made no mistakes at all. My boss got very agitated. "Is that all you've done? Here, take this!" He handed me a bottle of Geritol, a popular energy tonic. "You need it more than I do," he said. I was beginning to feel frustrated. My fingers were flying so fast the next day, I thought the typewriter keys would melt. But the harder I tried, the more mistakes I made. Finally I yelled, "This is driving me crazy!"

My boss looked up and quipped, "Short drive."

As usual, he proofread my work at three o'clock. At four, he wasn't upset as he had been all week. He just asked if I knew anyone who wanted a job.

I had to do something quickly. Man cannot live by bread alone, much less no bread at all. When I got home, angry at myself and fed up with life, it dawned on me that all week long I had not been paying the slightest attention to my dreams.

That night, as I lay in bed, I said out loud, "Dreams, I'm having a serious problem, so serious in fact, I don't even know what it is. I just can't seem to do anything right. If you can help, I promise to listen." To let my dreams know how serious I was, I laid a pen and open notebook at my bedside to write them down.

I awoke in a dream to find myself in a bowling alley. A tournament was under way, and here I was in front of hundreds of spectators, not to mention TV cameras, doing something I had not done more than three times in my entire waking life.

Immediately, it was my turn. The first two throws were consistent: both went straight into the gutter. The crowd roared with laughter. My turn to bowl came up again and again.

"A strike!" I would say to myself. "I've got to get a strike!" But the harder and faster I threw the ball, the quicker it tumbled into the gutter.

Of course, all the other contestants had been bowling since their first lifetime on earth. I was ready to give up and go home when the Living ECK Master, Harold Klemp, appeared beside me. He held a pair of binoculars.

"Here," he said. "I think you may need these."

"Very funny," I said.

"Don't be afraid," he replied. "Take a close look at those bowling pins."

He offered me the binoculars, and I took a peek. Sure enough, there was something I hadn't noticed before. Inscribed on each pin was a particular fear. One said, "Fear of Failure." Another read, "Fear of Ridicule." Another, "Fear of Rejection." Others included "Fear of the Unknown," "Fear of Making a Mistake," and "Fear of Not Being Absolutely Perfect." I turned to Harold and said, "These are the very fears I have been struggling with all my life."

"Really?" he said. "Well, here's your chance to get on top of the situation."

"How?"

"Very simple. Just imagine how you would honestly feel, on the surface and deep down, if these fears were cleared from your path. After all, they are really nothing more than dead images from the past, no more alive than those bowling pins."

"Thank you," I said, stepping up to the alley. When I picked up the ball, he said, "This is the ball of conscious thought. See the middle path?"

I looked down the alley to see a series of brilliant blue arrows running right down the middle. In the center of these arrows ran an almost invisible golden thread.

"Just release your conscious thought to the middle path and be neither for nor against what happens, for then you are truly trusting the ECK."

I released the ball to the straight and narrow, and bingo—a strike! Harold handed me a snapshot of the bottom of a shoe. Suddenly, I heard the piercing sound of a flute and woke up.

I was grateful for the experience, but the ending left me on edge. I began writing the dream in my notebook, but when I came to the picture of the bottom of a shoe, I was completely baffled.

After I wrote about the sound of the flute, my intuitive response was to reach for *The Flute of God,* an Eckankar book by Paul Twitchell. I grabbed the book off the dresser and just "happened" to open to these passages:

> You should have a good picture of the Real Self, the individual that is really you—Soul. . . . You must not let outer circumstances get so much of your attention and activity that you cannot pause, take time and lean upon the ECK power. . . . You are a part of the divine power so your thought forms a mold which the power instantly fills with life. Therefore, what you think with the whole of you, on the surface and deep down, inevitably comes to pass and manifests. . . . Belief in Spirit can take care of all things in the outer life. Life can be so relaxed, that it is a joyous possession. Many millions trust in Spirit and find the fulfillment of all their dreams.

From that day on, I was no longer Larry White, Mad Typist Desperate for Approval. I was simply Soul, the calm and fearless dreamer of isness, hereness, and nowness.

At first, I still made my share of mistakes, but when my boss commented on them, I viewed him as Soul and realized that, in a way, he had been seeing me as Soul all along. He had been aware of my full potential and now had motivated me to see it for myself.

I took my attention off making mistakes and placed it on just being Soul—working only for God, for the good of all. I learned the difference between pleasing people out of insecurity and serving God out of sincerity. Whenever fears popped up, I imagined they were nothing more than bowling pins and started throwing strikes.

The less I feared a mistake, the fewer mistakes I made. And within a few weeks, I got a raise and was promoted to full-time policy typist.

41

Dream Travel Can
Make Any Job Easier

Rae Franceschini

ave you ever been so nervous or anxious about a new job that you almost quit before Day One? I had been at the same job for nearly nine years when I decided on a complete career change. Twelve-hour days pared down to six; five days a week down to three. The biggest change was going from sitting all day to standing.

The interview went well, and my new employer and I agreed on the day I was to start. But now, a whole new fear gripped me. How well would I do my new tasks?

The job was in a cookie store. I had baked a lot at home and knew how to cook, yet this was different: two large ovens, three tall racks for cooling trays of cookies, huge tubs for dough, and on and on. It dawned on me that each day we would be making nine different kinds of cookies. How would I master all this?

Immediately, I became very nervous. It wasn't long before I considered calling the owner to back out. Finally, as my fear peaked, I let my inner awareness surface long enough to say, "Hey, wait a minute! Give yourself a break. Put a little trust in your inner guidance; you might be fine."

I did stop fretting but wondered: *Had that been* my *voice? Did I really believe I could do this job well?*

By now it was late Friday night, time for bed. I set my fear aside and took a few deep breaths. I asked the Mahanta to help me cope with the days ahead and give me the inner strength to give the new job my best.

In the dream state that evening, the Mahanta took me to the cookie store. I knew it was late, but the lights were on and no one was there. In the dream, I started to explore the shop. I looked under the counters, opened drawers, and checked cupboards. I saw where all the paper goods were kept and the ingredients for making dough. I noted which supplies were kept in the walk-in freezer and how things were done. Getting familiar with the shop really set me at ease. I finished my night's sleep peacefully.

What an incredible opportunity I had been given. I awoke early Saturday with a clear and total recall, and immediately thanked the Mahanta. For the rest of the weekend, I didn't give the new job another thought. All I could do was my best, and after that, I could learn.

The following Tuesday was my first day. The person training me was really more interested in the fact that it was her last day. In her excitement, she reviewed my tasks too quickly. I watched and listened. When it was time for my trainer to leave, my other new coworker became nervous. Was she going to have to do all the work alone for the day, with me in the way?

I saw the dread in her eyes as I set to work, pulling tools out of drawers and running out back for ingredients. I asked her to make dough, remarking that as soon as she had it done, I'd start dropping the cookies. I continued to arrange things in the store as if I had already been working there for many months, instead of hours.

She looked at me and asked, "How do you know where everything is?" I said, "Sometimes you just have to trust your inner feelings. Now I'm really going to need your help, if we're to get all this work done today."

We started making cookies, and a few hours later we finished ahead of schedule. She was surprised but happy to have me working with her.

I left work with the most wonderful feeling. Thanks to the Mahanta, I got through Day One and took a giant step in self-confidence and awareness.

42

A Gift to Remember

Fran Blackwell

When I was nine years old, I began having visits in my dreams from an old Asian man. He had a long white beard and the most beautiful eyes. They seemed to look right through me. He wore a funny little hat on his head and had a beautiful smile. Every night he would talk to me about life and explain the meaning of different things I wondered about.

One afternoon I went to a movie with my girlfriends. We were standing in line waiting to buy our tickets, laughing and being silly like normal nine-year-old girls. Suddenly I felt something. I looked past the booth where they sold the tickets. There stood the man who had been in my dreams for almost a year. When our eyes met, he nodded at me. Then he was gone.

I didn't think to turn around to my girlfriends and say, "Look at that man over there! He is the man from my dreams!" For some reason it seemed best to keep silent.

That very night he came to me again in my dreams. He said, "Tonight will be the last time I meet with you. I have to leave you now. I have to go away."

I replied, "Oh, but I'm going to miss you! I wish you didn't have to leave."

He said, "I have to do what I have to do, but just so you know that dreams are real, I have a gift for you." He placed a white plastic barrette in my hand and curled my fingers around it. Then he was gone.

When I woke up the next morning, the white barrette was really in my hand!

I began thinking about my parents, especially my mother. If she saw me with this barrette she would want to know where it came from. She wouldn't understand that a man in my dreams gave it to me. Before anyone else awoke, I snuck out of the house. I went out to the backyard, dug a hole, and buried the barrette.

But I only let go of the barrette's physical aspect. The true meaning of the gift never left me. That gift gave me the understanding of the true reality of our inner and outer lives. It proved that dreams are real.

I'll never forget the wonderful man who taught me in my dreams. At the time, I didn't know his name. Years later when I found the teachings of Eckankar, I discovered he was the ancient Chinese ECK Master Lai Tsi.

43

The Root Cause

Uwe Reisenleiter

*D*ivine Spirit uses everything around us to teach us about ourselves. For me, that means computers—computers at work and computers at home.

One evening I was loading software into a newly acquired home computer when I noticed an incomplete statement in one of the files that the machine uses to start itself. Spelling is not one of my strengths, and computers are notoriously unforgiving when it comes to poor spelling. When this computer read the revised (but sadly misspelled) file, it simply stopped. It took me many hours to finally accept that I didn't have the skill to repair my mistake.

The next morning the right person with the right tools and expertise fixed the problem in a couple of minutes. But there was more to come.

Part two of this experience began at work the following morning when I turned on my reliable office computer. It also refused to start up. What was Divine Spirit, the ECK, trying to tell me? Was this a waking dream that held a message for my spiritual benefit?

The commands that set up and prepare a computer to run programs reside in something called the *root directory*. In both cases, I reasoned, computer failure had been caused by corrupted or missing files in this root directory. And in both cases these files had to be rewritten or replaced. This had never happened to me before!

I thought about the spiritual message in this experience. Then it hit me.

As I unfold spiritually, I need to look at the root of myself—my own root directory. With the help of the Mahanta, my inner guide, I need to replace or rewrite files—those attitudes that defeat my spiritual goals—with ones that support my goals, so that I can meet life with an open heart. By doing this, I am aware of the tools God is using to teach me about myself, and I see that the ECK resides at the root of all.

44

How God Answered Me

Becky Williams

As a young girl, I was very sensitive. One of five siblings, I found there wasn't a lot of love to go around in my unstable family. I often felt alone and afraid, like a child in the wilderness. But every night before going to sleep, I made a connection with a very loving presence, which I thought was God.

We would "talk," and I would feel God's love and reassurance wrap around me like a warm blanket. Sometimes I would dream of being in a room filled with the most wonderful, luminous, soft blue light.

As I grew up, I forgot this very special relationship. The drama of everyday life captured all my attention. Life continued to be a little bumpy for me, but when I turned twenty-three things really sped up.

My relationship with my boyfriend ended abruptly when he was transferred to another state. I was brokenhearted. I was also just starting a new career, barely getting by financially. And a difficult relationship with a coworker made it hard to go to work each day. Things got even worse when the water pipes in my little cottage apartment froze and burst on an unusually cold night.

So I found myself sleeping on a friend's couch in a miserable frame of mind. I lay staring at the ceiling, with the weight of the world on my heart. Every source of comfort or love had been stripped away. Once again I felt like a child in the wilderness.

Suddenly I remembered my forgotten connection with God of long ago.

My spirits lifted a bit with memory of the love and reassurance I had found in the presence of Divine Spirit. It had been very real then. Now it was my only hope. As I fell asleep, I asked God to come to me as in my childhood.

I fell into a fitful dream: I was walking through a house in chaos. People were arguing, and pots were boiling over. Each room was worse than the next. The rooms seemed to symbolize my life. Finally I announced to the other occupants that I was going outside to find help. I ran barefoot through the snow until I came to a man who stood by a fork in the road at the base of a mountain. One road ran past, while the other went straight up the mountain.

Hurriedly, I asked the man which way I should go for help. Without saying a word he pointed up the side of the mountain. Not wanting to waste time, I quickly began my ascent.

The next thing I knew, I was at the very top, holding on with my arms wrapped around the peak. There was a wind, although I don't recall really feeling it.

My attention was off in the distance, riveted on an incredible ball of white light.

As the light drew closer, I felt myself wrapped in a peaceful, loving warmth beyond all imagination. Time, space, and even my memory were suspended. I remember simply that I dwelled in divine love.

While I was there it seemed like eternity, but all too soon this presence communicated to me that it was time to go back to my earth life.

I resisted at first. How could I leave such serenity and joy? Finally, I began my descent, with this loving presence beside me. We reached a plateau, where I could see the affairs of my life laid out like pieces of a giant puzzle.

Silently I saw how to fit them back together. I was amazed at how much easier it was from this viewpoint!

When I reached the bottom of the mountain, many of the characters from my life were there to greet me. I remember in particular seeing the face of my difficult coworker. She had a grin on her face that acknowledged the humor and absurdity of life. Her smile awoke me from the dream.

I just lay there on my friend's couch with the amazing realization that my cry had been answered. And although I didn't know it then, the deep pain and loss I had been experiencing in my life was making room for a greater love to come in.

One week after my dream, I was having lunch with a young school-aged girl from an underprivileged home. I was a volunteer in a special program and would often take her for weekend outings.

My young friend noticed our waiter's unusual blue medallion. She asked him what it meant. He replied simply, "The Light and Sound of God."

A jolt of recognition went through my body! If he had chosen any other words to describe the meaning of the ⊕ pendant he wore, it probably would have escaped my attention. But with my dream fresh in mind, I blurted out that I had to know more. Could I come back later to talk?

He agreed, and for the next two weeks I came almost daily to ask him about this teaching called Eckankar. He explained that the soft blue light I had seen as a child was the presence of my inner guide, the Mahanta.

So began my incredible journey back up the mountain of God on the path of Eckankar. Now nearly twelve years have passed. My inner and outer life has healed and grown beyond anything I could have imagined. I continue to be amazed that the protection and love of my inner guide, the Mahanta, has been with me all my life.

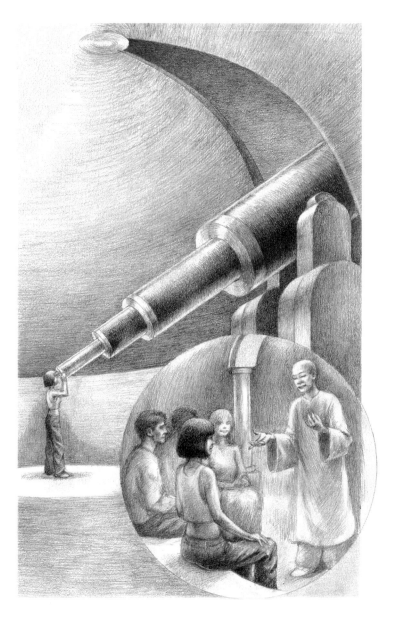

Your dreams are like a telescope that can give a better view of something that is normally out of your reach: your spiritual side.

45

Tips on How to Interpret Your Dreams

Harold Klemp

reams—the stuff of wonder, fear, the un-known—are always certain to pique our curiosity.

Dreams were the reason for the good fortune of Joseph of the Old Testament. He overcame all odds—treachery by his brothers, slavery, and imprisonment—to rise in stature and power until he was second only to the mighty pharaoh of Egypt.

Dreams hold an aura of mystery. They give power to anyone who can—or claims to—interpret them. Elias Howe, inventor of the sewing machine, tried for years to develop his invention, but without success. Until, in a dream, he got orders to finish it or pay with his life. Strong motivation, indeed.

Among the many examples of the influence of dreams, there is the one of Samuel Clemens, the American humorist known as Mark Twain. He foresaw the death of his brother Henry, who also worked on the riverboats of the Mississippi River during the 1850s. One night, Twain awoke from a nightmare in which he saw the metal coffin of his brother. On it lay a bouquet of white flowers, a red rose in the middle. A few weeks later, his brother suffered severe injuries from a boiler explosion on the river. He died shortly after.

Upon his arrival a few days later, Twain found the setting exactly as it had appeared in his dream. Some people had taken pity upon his brother and had collected money to buy an expensive metal coffin, instead of the wooden boxes usually used in river accidents. As Twain paid his last respects, a woman entered the room and placed on the coffin a bouquet of white flowers with a single red rose in the middle.

Dreams touch every level of our life. They may let us glimpse the future, or give suggestions for healing, or share insights into our relationships. Above all, they can and will steer us more directly toward God.

What is this fantasy about dreams?

First, understand that the dream world is anything but a fantasy. A "confused" dream simply shows the inability of our mind to accept truth head-on, so it bends the facts and artfully weaves them into a story line that is less likely to cause us distress. Yes, dreams are real.

A mother listening to her young daughter tell of an inner experience from the night before dismissed it offhand as only a dream. The girl quickly corrected her. "Not just a dream, Mom," she said. "It was real."

So, first, understand that the land of dreams is an actual place. Second, any experience you gain in the dream world is as useful to you spiritually as any of those you may have here in the human body.

To grasp the universal nature of dreams, take a step back and imagine that you are standing at the top of all worlds. The identity that can do that, to command a view even of creation itself, is the real you—eternal Soul. Soul is a child of God, and, by nature, godlike. And so It can share in the divine attributes of wisdom, joy, freedom, and divine love.

So why doesn't It? Why don't you?

Your dreams are like a telescope that can give a better view of something that is normally out of reach: your spiritual side. That includes how you act, feel, reflect, think, react, and even love. Most people fear putting the telescope of dreams to their eye, afraid of what they might see.

So what about interpreting dreams? Where do the beginners start? Do they begin in the bookstore, buying volumes of books that supposedly give the inside scoop on dreams?

No. That's not to say they won't learn something by reading books on dreams, because they will. They will learn the many ways that people approach the dream world: through symbols, the emotions, as outer causes, or as riddles. These only give a small part of the picture. If people have the wisdom and insight, and spend enough time at it, they can eventually piece all the odd ends together and come up with their own dream patchwork of sorts.

Yet it will still miss the beauty and wonder of *living,* in full consciousness, in your heavens of dreams.

Dreams have a meaning at every step—the human, emotional, causal, mental, subconscious, and spiritual levels. They correspond to the six planes of existence, spoken of so often in the ECK works—the Physical, Astral, Causal, Mental, Etheric, and Soul Planes. And each deals with a part of us. Each of our dreams comes mainly from one of these areas.

Our task is to keep the interpretation of dreams simple.

Look at each dream in one of three levels. They are about our daily life, our emotions and thoughts, and, less often, about the pure spiritual side. So, simply put, there are dreams about our everyday events, our emotional well-being, and our relationship with God.

The beauty of dreams is that they go with you everywhere, no matter what. They are a portable treasure. You need only recall them, to recognize them as a divine gift to gain insight into your true spiritual nature. Never are you without your dreams.

Is it possible to go somewhere for the weekend and say, "Oh, I forgot to pack my dreams"?

No, they are always with you, because they are a part of you and you of them. They give a broader picture of yourself and the great spiritual potential that lies within you.

I would say that some figures of state, church, and science understate the value of dreams, for they often ridicule or punish those who speak too freely about the dream life. A dreamer is often an independent being. He looks inwardly, instead of outwardly, for the real answers to life.

My plan for this article was to give a sample of dreams and explain them, but there are already many such examples in this book and in the ECK dream discourses. This is a chance to speak directly to your heart, to you as Soul.

Here, then, are a few thoughts on how to enter a better spiritual life through the doorway of dreams:

1. Dream—get plenty of rest for a few days. Then go to sleep with the intention of remembering some of the places you visit while your human self lies sleeping. (It helps to write the dreams down as soon as you awaken.)

2. Interpret your dreams—ask the Dream Master (my inner self) to let you see each dream on three levels: the daily, the emotional/mental, and the spiritual.

3. Realize your dreams—take the dream lessons and apply them to your everyday life.

You can make this study of dreams as easy as you like. However, you need to give the ECK Dream Master permission to help you understand them.

Your consent can be as simple as saying, "Please, Harold, help me remember my dreams and understand them."

It's that easy.

If you want your dreams to lift you into a higher state of awareness and joy, you have only to ask. My task is to help you become mindful of yourself in the real worlds, the dreamlands of God.

I'll see you in your dreams.

Part Three

Soul Travel

It is Soul's relationship to God that gives meaning
to life. It is the golden tie that binds.

46

Just Where Does God Fit In?

Harold Klemp

A wonderful gentleman, a member of Eckankar
for over twenty-five years, wrote a letter of
good spiritual insight to me around the
Christmas holiday season.

First, he reflected upon *Stranger by the River.* This
book, by Paul Twitchell, is a dialogue between a spiritual seeker and his Master in another time and another place. Twenty-five years ago, this gentleman had
dismissed it as being simple and without depth. Yet the
book deals with the issues of this world: love, wisdom,
life and death, the nature of God and Soul, and others.
Those issues are not simple.

Now he has come to a startling realization: he has
changed dramatically in his own state of consciousness
since then as a member of Eckankar. How did he come
to know of the change?

About twenty-five years ago, he gave his first intro-
ductory talk on the teachings of ECK. The audience was
sizeable, about thirty-five people. Like any good con-
vert, this gentleman spoke with conviction about a
popular subject then—Soul Travel. He went on and on.

Near the end of his talk, a man at the back of the
room raised his hand. "And just where does God fit into
all of this?" he asked.

This question set the speaker back on his heels, because he realized he himself had missed the whole point of the ECK teachings. So how could he lecture others?

Soul Travel, dreams, past lives, the ancient science of prophecy, healing, and especially love are all part of the ECK teachings, of course. However, they do not stand alone. They must always be taken in the whole context of Soul's relationship to God. It is this relationship that gives meaning to life. It is the golden tie that binds.

So how did this gentleman learn about his own change of consciousness during the last twenty-five years?

During the most recent Christmas holiday season, he was walking through a shopping mall. The place was full of Christmas decorations. All around him, harried shoppers were flitting from store to store in an attempt to complete their last-minute shopping. Even the piped-in music was urgent. Shop till you drop.

Now he asked himself the same question the man in the back of the lecture room had asked him twenty-five years ago, *And just where does God fit into all of this?*

He reflected upon the chaos around him.

Christmas comes from two words: *Christ* (a state of consciousness) and *mass* (a worship service or celebration). Wasn't Christmas to be a time for Christians to give thanks to God and show gratitude for all the blessings they had received? Wasn't it a season to return a bit of God's love through offerings of charity and service, to reflect divine love in some way to those around them?

But the shopping mall was a commercial circus.

"What are you going to give me?" and "What am I to get for you?"

This gentleman observed the chaos around him. He had taken a table in the food court of the mall to have a cup of coffee. Half-joking, he asked a young man next to him, "I wonder what God would think of all this?"

"What has God to do with it?" replied the young man.

Our friend went home. In his own way, twenty-five years ago he himself had been like that young man. The teachings about Soul Travel, dreams, past lives, the ancient science of prophecy, healing, and especially love are all meaningless unless taken in the context of God's love for Soul. The same holds true for Christmas.

This gentleman reached for *Stranger by the River* and opened it at random. In "The Law of Life" (chapter 31), the ECK Master Rebazar Tarzs reminded him: "When you are full of opinions and speculations, God is withdrawn from thee."

In other words, live and let live.

A dear friend of ours could perhaps ask the question too: "And just where does God fit into all of this?"

He is a successful businessman. Yet lately, a severe drop in the value of his home forced him to sell it at a loss. At the same time a business venture failed. Like so many other successful people, the byways of his life show a lot of losses—certainly not the string of unbroken successes that other people finally view at the end of a long life of ups and downs.

So currently, our friend has had a few downs in a row. Such an experience is likely to get an individual looking only at past failures, instead of seeing all the areas where his life is blessed: health, a family, love for God and life (despite all recent reverses), and optimism in spite of it all.

His thoughts therefore took a trip down memory

lane. Since current losses are so much a part of his life for now, he naturally found his mind searching out earlier losses.

One such experience was a heartbreaker. Especially for a youth.

As a young boy, he had a paper route. To boost subscriptions, the publisher held a contest for the paperboys. The boy who got the most new subscribers to the newspaper in a given period of time would win a trip to Hawaii with his parents.

Our young hero worked hard. So by closing time on the last day of the competition, he had won by turning in thirteen more "starts" than any of the other paperboys. He could just see himself in Hawaii. His proud parents would politely tell any and all who would listen, "Our son won this trip for us by selling newspapers!"

However, there was a small matter of backyard (barnyard?) politics that he hadn't counted on. His chief competitor's father likely had a friend in the publisher's office who passed along the end-of-day totals to him. After all, the expenditure of so much money for three tickets to Hawaii might as well be used to return a favor to a personal friend of someone at the newspaper. Why waste them on just any kid?

Whatever happened is not known.

Somehow, though, his competitor's father learned that our friend was ahead by thirteen starts. So, after hours—after the close of the contest—the father bought twenty newspaper subscriptions for friends and relatives. Then he slipped them through the door of the publisher's office. At night. Someone there approved the illegal subscriptions, and our friend's competitor and his parents got the free trip to Hawaii.

To make matters worse, second prize was a one-speed bike. At a time when three-speed bikes were popular, no self-respecting boy wanted to be seen on a one-speed.

Ashes heaped upon dirt.

A good question for a young boy to ask, "I wonder what God would think of all this?"

Rebazar Tarzs, in *Stranger by the River,* might have answered Soul like this, as he once did the seeker: "Thy experience is nothing less than thy own choices and thoughts made visible" ("The Law of the Self," chapter 12).

Had the boy counted his chicks before they were hatched? Or had his competitor's dishonest father received some sort of tip and special considerations to pay off someone's debt to him?

In the end, does it matter?

Earth is a schoolroom. We're here to have every possible experience. That's how Soul finds spiritual purification and becomes godlike in the end. Why are you here? To make money and get rich? Maybe. There is certainly nothing wrong with money, but what's the use of having it while learning nothing about your spiritual purpose here on earth?

Once more, as Rebazar tells the seeker, "You, yourself, are your own problem. You must understand and act to solve the mystery of thy little self before you can solve the mystery of God."

47

Helping My Father
across the Veil

Carol Andrew

I was longing to return to England to visit my family. I felt a sense of urgency to visit Dad, even though I couldn't figure out why. At eighty-six, he was very spry, the chief organizer of the community center dance club.

My family was on my mind as my partner, Tom, and I prepared to drive from north Florida to Minneapolis for the annual ECK Summer Festival (an Eckankar seminar) and to visit the Temple of ECK in Chanhassen, Minnesota. As we headed out of town Tom remembered we had forgotten something and slowed to make a U-turn. The turn took us past a previously hidden billboard: "London Round-Trip—$389.00."

I wondered at the timing. Was this the guiding hand of Divine Spirit, moving me toward England?

After the seminar when I arrived back home, I found a message from my sister in England. Dad was seriously ill and in the hospital. In the morning, I immediately booked a flight to London.

When I arrived, it seemed it was Dad's time to leave. During a spiritual exercise that evening, I asked Sri Harold Klemp, the Mahanta, if I could be there to help when Dad crossed over to the worlds beyond the physical.

Later as I sat at Dad's bedside, I sensed a tall, cloaked figure at the foot of his bed. It leaned over to Dad as if to gather him up. This was the Grim Reaper, the Angel of Death.

The being moved back to the foot of the bed. Four globes of radiant, golden light suddenly stationed themselves around Dad's room, like sentries.

All this I sensed rather than saw with physical eyes, but it was more real than my five senses. When Tom walked into the room later, he also saw a tall, cloaked being waiting at the foot of the bed and a sentry of light in each corner!

Just hours after we left for the night, the hospital called to let me know Dad had died. I was very upset, but I sat down quietly and began my spiritual exercise. As I sang HU, I could feel the loving presence of the Mahanta, my guide, comforting me and helping me focus.

It was difficult to connect at first; I felt Dad was resisting death with all his might. Finally I saw him. He was with the tall cloaked being, flying into a long, narrow tube or tunnel that sloped sharply downward. I followed and found Dad lying in an ungainly heap at the bottom. The look of indignation on his face made me chuckle.

"C'mon Dad," I said, extending a hand.

Awareness flooded his face as he stood. For the first time in years, he was free from arthritis pain. He rolled his once-frozen shoulders in delight: "Look, they work!"

Then he asked, "Why are you here? And how did you get here?" I explained Eckankar had taught me how to Soul Travel in the worlds beyond the physical, and that I had come because I love him. He was as delighted as a child.

We began to move up a ramp of golden light, toward an indescribably huge and brilliant white light. A beautiful being came forward and extended her arms. "Hello, Stan!" It was a youthful version of my mother, who had died almost twenty years ago. On earth, my parents had endured a difficult relationship. Seeing her gift of unconditional love filled me with peaceful joy.

Just as the light started to engulf us, I was held back. Dad and Mum disappeared into God's pure love for all Souls.

I thanked the cloaked being and gave the ancient benediction "Baraka Bashad," which means "May the blessings be." He bowed graciously and vanished.

When I returned to the physical consciousness and left the bedroom, I found Tom standing in the hallway with a big grin. He hugged me and exclaimed, "I watched you in a spiritual exercise of my own!"

"At first your Dad just stood there in his usual confrontational, Royal-Air-Force-Sergeant posture," Tom reported. "Then you arrived and zoomed down into a narrow tunnel with him. I was about to follow when one of those egg-shaped balls of light stopped me."

Tom's testimony offered valuable confirmation that this experience was not some wild fantasy. And I was grateful the Inner Master allowed me to share this one last, great journey of love with my father.

48

Spiritual Breakthrough!

John Hammontree

*A*bout two months after I became a member of Eckankar, I was at home, sitting in my recliner doing my spiritual exercises, when I fell asleep. All of a sudden I entered a semiconscious state of awareness that was familiar. This was the state I'd experienced often—my entire life—but it had always terrified me.

This time it didn't. I just lay back, relaxed, and started to sing HU, a love song to God.

When I sat up, my physical body stayed where it was in the recliner. Excited, I thought, *I've finally done it! I've gotten out of my body with Soul Travel!* I was thrilled beyond words.

I suddenly thought, *I'd like to go visit my niece.* The next thing I knew, I was whizzing off at incredible speed. Seconds later I arrived at a house I'd never seen before. I went in through a front window and landed very softly. A multicolored cat scampered away, aware that I was there. I got my bearings then started walking around, looking for my niece. I took two steps forward, then just as fast I wound up back in my body.

Later I called my niece and told her what had happened. She verified my description of her house. Then she told me the cat I saw was her favorite pet,

Muffin, who had recently passed over.

This was an experience I'll always treasure. Recently, I had the opportunity to visit my niece in Sacramento, California, and her home was exactly as I saw it during Soul Travel.

49

The Sacred Reaper

Joann Shelton

*E*ager for an out-of-body experience, I sat down in the den and opened my new book on the subject. I read the instructions carefully, then shut my eyes and blocked out the sound of the television.

Immediately I was in a foreign land—vivid and colorful.

About a hundred yards in front of me, a man worked on a steep, green-terraced hillside. He wore a robe and a pale yellow, pointed straw hat which obscured his face. I watched his arms move rhythmically as he tilled his rice. He seemed not to notice me.

Then the reality of the experience hit me. *I really am here,* I thought. Instantly I was back in the den with my roommates, the dog, and the blaring television.

A search for answers to this dramatic event only brought more questions. My own religion didn't offer any answers so I turned to various spiritual teachings. I learned about dreams and reincarnation, but I couldn't find a satisfactory explanation of what had happened to me.

Then I found a book which told all about how the universe works. Each page revealed ideas I immediately understood and accepted. This book,

ECKANKAR—The Key to Secret Worlds by Paul Twitchell, the modern-day founder of Eckankar, explained conscious out-of-the body experiences, or Soul Travel.

I learned I had traveled to another plane of existence in my Soul body. I was ecstatic. I wanted to know more about Eckankar and the people who believed in it. I called a number in the phone book and learned an Eckankar seminar was being held nearby. I decided to attend.

The first thing I noticed when I walked in the door was an art exhibit. I stepped up to view the art and was astonished to see a painting of the very same man I had seen in my Soul Travel experience. His golden straw hat and shoulders hunched over his work were portrayed from exactly the opposite point of view from mine.

I stood mesmerized before the painting. A man walked up and asked if he could help me.

"Did you paint this?" I asked.

The man nodded. "Yes."

"I've seen this man."

"Yes, many others have seen him too. I painted him, but I don't know who he is."

I thanked the artist and walked away. This seeming coincidence confirmed I really was in the right place at the right time.

I never learned the identity of the man in the painting, but it really doesn't matter. By trying a spiritual exercise, I had opened the door to the daily adventure of walking in these divine worlds. Just one journey into those worlds brought me a great gift—the understanding that life really exists beyond this physical plane.

50

Mahanta's Golden Smile

Jim Jackson

On the last day of February my sister, Phyllis, died. She had been an invalid for over thirty years. Our parents had cared for her in their home for sixteen years. Then they became physically unable to manage her care, and she was placed in a nursing home.

After my dad phoned me at my dental office, I silently sang HU a few times and spoke to the Inner Master, the Mahanta. If it would not interfere with anyone's spiritual growth, I asked, would he please help my sister during this transitional stage?

A few minutes later, as I was taking a dental impression, I gazed out the window at the green trees and clear blue sky, thinking of Phyllis. Suddenly, I was in a world far away from the dental office, and I got confirmation of my prayers being answered.

It was a beautiful dark-blue world. Thousands of globes of lights clustered in the background. I could see a faint white image of the Mahanta walking along a path toward the masses of lights. He had one arm around another globe of light. I knew this was the dear Soul who had been my sister in this lifetime.

As they passed, the Mahanta, Wah Z, turned his head and looked at me, giving me a big smile. The silent inner communication said: "All is going well and as it should be."

Then I was back in the physical awareness. The whole experience took only moments, but it gave me at least two lifetimes of love and gratitude.

A day of sadness was transformed by a smile into one of joy, love, caring, and thankfulness.

51

The Search for My Other Self

Cameron Fox

One night in 1967 I wearily went up to my room after having put all the children to bed. My husband was out of town. I sat in bed with my back against the wall and shut my eyes to just let the thoughts flow freely.

Suddenly I found myself in a room that was not familiar to me. There was a bed in it, and a person in the bed. With a shock, I realized the person resembled me. About three feet above the bed hovered another body, a sparkling blue body!

There was also a form in the corner of the room, and it had a bright blue-white color to it. I stood there completely baffled. There was no fear, but I was curious what was going on.

From the corner, the blue form said, "Cameron, what is the word?"

The being waited for my answer. I said, "God." My voice echoed around the room—God, God, God. The sound became a thousand beautiful notes swirling around me.

The blue form faded, and suddenly I was standing in the doorway of my bedroom. I looked at my body sitting up with my back to the wall. How was I supposed to get back into it? I couldn't think of anything to do but try to sit on this physical shell. I did this and promptly shifted into a waking state.

I couldn't sleep for the rest of the night—but I wasn't even tired the next day. I felt wonderful! And if I was going crazy, it didn't keep me from doing my chores and chatting with the neighbors just like always.

I sat down in the cool of the afternoon shade to watch the children play in the yard. I felt a tremendous urge to pray. "If I need to know the answers to what has been happening to me, God, please send me to the right person," I whispered.

The only answer I got was an inner nudge. "Go read a book." I wasn't pleased with this revelation, because books had been of no help so far in my search for spiritual information.

I went into the study. The bookcase was filled with volumes on philosophy, religion, psychology, and literature. But the book that jumped out at me was a shortened version of *Aladdin or the Wonderful Lamp,* an old Persian tale. I'd always enjoyed the *Arabian Nights* as a child.

As I read, the tale took on a new meaning. I realized that the bottle represented my physical body. The strong, all-knowing genie that came out represented the other self. I must have read it over a dozen times in the next few days, looking for more clues. Other self was the name I had given to that higher being I was seeking.

Fairy tales took on new significance. *Peter Pan* was the boy that never grew old. Did this author have an understanding of the other self? Alice in Wonderland was transported to a strange land; Dorothy in *The Wonderful Wizard of Oz* visited a land "over the rainbow."

This was all interesting—but it didn't really tell me

about my other self. The feeling of expectation was great. I didn't know what I was expecting, but it was always there. I continued to study, work part-time, and take care of my family, but always there was the feeling that something grand was headed my way.

I spent some time each day in a form of meditation. I would select a passage from a great book such as the Bible, *The Bhagavad Gita*, or an inspiring book of poetry. I would go over it in my mind and then sit and see what entered my inner vision. This seemed to sharpen my mental skills. My memory of what I had read improved rapidly. I felt great excitement over learning almost anything and everything.

Still, there was scarcely any information about the other self. I had just about given up hope.

About this time, a special person began to appear to me after my meditative exercises. I thought I was daydreaming. But one day when I opened my eyes and got up from the floor where I had been sitting, he was still there. He appeared in a blue form.

The next day he appeared as I was walking down the hall of my house. I thought he was a ghost and approached him boldly, because I'd just read a book about haunted English castles. "What do you want?" I asked him. He only smiled. "Go away," I told him severely.

Several months went by. I could not get the blue man's accepting smile and clear, knowing eyes out of my mind.

One day as I lay across the end of the bed I felt a vibration shake my entire body. I tried to cry out, but my voice did not make any sound. Suddenly I found myself standing by the bed.

Then the doorbell rang. When I went downstairs to open it, my hand went right through the door! I went back upstairs, and the man in the blue form was there.

He said, "Follow me."

I felt excited and ready for something—I didn't know what. The experience dissolved.

Several weeks lapsed. I asked the person to return, but he didn't. I started having strange dreams of going into a temple. There was a large book there. When I opened it, the page had only one letter on it: *V.* This dream repeated itself for many months.

Each time the dream ended, I was given a word that did not mean anything to me at the time—*Vairag.* I could not find it in any dictionary.

About that time, I was introduced to a retired Catholic priest by a neighbor. He had had several out-of-body experiences during a heart attack. Someone had told him of a man in Las Vegas that knew about Soul Travel. He couldn't get any answers from the church, so he went to Las Vegas. He came back with a picture of a man. It was the same man that had appeared to me! His name was Paul Twitchell, the founder of Eckankar. I was both relieved and excited.

That night I asked Paul Twitchell to appear. I was taken to a lovely garden in the dream state and escorted around by someone who said I was an old friend—but this man had a dark beard. I would later come to know him as the ECK Master Rebazar Tarzs.

I was hungry to learn more about this strange religion that Paul Twitchell taught called Eckankar. But I didn't have the money to travel to Las Vegas. Besides, whenever I talked about it to my husband, he would get angry. My mind worked hard to put my recent experiences out of sight so I could go on with life.

About that time, my husband and I made plans to move to another state. Soon I started having regular experiences with out-of-body travel—a term I learned from my friend the priest. At night I could fly over the houses in my neighborhood or go into town. I could read a book and go to the places described just by closing my eyes and relaxing. Just for fun, I sent for some books and written material on Eckankar. I really wasn't overly interested in reading about Soul Travel because I was doing it. What could anyone teach me anyway? I had come this far by myself.

One day everyone was gone for the afternoon but me. Sitting in the midst of books and packing boxes, I closed my eyes to review all of my experiences in the last year. I wondered if I would still have them in our new home. Then it happened—Mr. Twitchell appeared to me just like a neighbor coming to visit. He stood in the doorway, lit from behind by a brilliant light that made it hard for me to look directly at him.

"I will teach you," he said calmly.

I stared at him for a minute and then gasped, "What?"

"I will teach you more about Soul Travel."

I wanted to tell him how much I already knew. "I could fly right over the houses now, if I wanted to," I said.

He stepped forward, and the light around him intensified. "Any bird can do that," he said. Then he left.

I felt humbled by his presence. I wept with disappointment at my arrogance. When I went to get the mail that day, I found a surprise. I had received my first monthly discourse on Eckankar.

My search for the other self had ended. In a thousand different ways over the years, as a member of Eckankar I would learn how to become that other self. I am Soul.

I learned about myself as a spiritual entity, that we live forever, why I'd lost my physical leg, and that I had other, nonphysical bodies: the Emotional, Mental, Causal, Etheric, and Soul forms.

52

An Out-of-Body Healing

Gaston Ouellet

In 1978 I had a severe accident while working for a railroad out near an Indian reservation. I was crushed between two train cars and lost one leg just below the knee. Just after the impact, my coworkers laid me on the ground, and I was instantly out of the body.

Two beings met me in that other dimension, and one of them said, "Come this way, I want to show you something."

They led me to an unusual temple. I spent forty-eight hours drifting in and out of consciousness, as they taught me. I learned about myself as a spiritual entity, that we live forever, why I'd lost my physical leg, and that I had other, nonphysical bodies: the Emotional, Mental, Causal, Etheric, and Soul forms.

Before I woke up, the beings said, "We will always be with you. Only now we will come to you in the dream state, to remind you of what you've learned."

For the next three weeks in the hospital, they met me in the inner worlds every time I fell asleep. I never paid much attention to this experience. I thought it was related to the heavy sedatives the doctors gave me. I didn't share the experience with many people.

At the end of the three weeks, they told me they

215

would continue to teach me in "light form." The dreams stopped, but I began to see little sparkling lights out of the corner of my vision. It was disturbing, but I still attributed it to sedative aftereffects.

Four days later I met a Blackfoot Indian family. They worked as trappers and invited me to go with them into the wilderness the following year if I got myself an artificial limb.

The following year I was guided back up to the mountains for more spiritual and physical healing. I met the family again and began a wilderness adventure with their dog team, tepee, log house, and canoes.

One afternoon I was outside working on the log house and overheard them singing a word called *HU.* I ran inside and told them how beautiful it was, and to please continue. They sounded so beautiful together. The father went and got a book called *The Shariyat-Ki-Sugmad.* "If you like the music," he grinned, "maybe you should read the book. These are the scriptures of Eckankar."

Every night they sat around the lanterns and read to each other from many different books. But I never paid much attention. "I don't believe you find answers in a religious book," I scoffed. "There's no truth in them. Truth is inside."

"Well," he smiled, "I agree. But let me put it this way: You have nothing to lose. You're in the middle of the wilderness."

The first words I read when I opened the book were "the first section of these works, which was dictated by Fubbi Quantz, the great ECK Master who serves at the Katsupari Monastery in northern Tibet."

A feeling of strange familiarity came over me. I yelled to the father, "I know this, I know this exactly! I've been to this monastery, I know what this is."

All the family started rejoicing, they were so happy. The father went to the house to get pictures of the ECK Masters.

When he showed them to me, I instantly recognized one of the beings who had helped me when I lost my leg. His name was Rebazar Tarzs. From that moment on, I became a follower of Eckankar.

Without the ECK Masters' guidance, my accident would have led me into such a dark place. Instead, it brought me the light of truth.

53

Love Always Finds a Way

Dorothy M. Weiss

opened the door, and there stood my dad. "Hello, Dorothy Marie. I just came to see how you're doing."

He looked wonderful! I was so glad to see him; I fell into his arms, feeling the familiar strength of his shoulders. He threw his head back and laughed. I clasped his hand, babbling joyously, telling him everything. Words unspoken for years tumbled out. "I love you, Dad, and I'm grateful for all you did. I regret not spending more time with you; I took you for granted. I could have been more understanding, done more to help you."

In the soft golden glow of the room, I talked with my father, basking in his smile, the warmth of his love, holding his hand.

Then a telephone rang. As I turned away to answer it, my father disappeared. Dazed, I looked at the receiver in my hand. I told the caller I would call back. I placed the telephone in its cradle, and slowly began to review this experience.

Today would have been my father's birthday. He died many years ago. On this special day I had decided to do a spiritual exercise. As I sang HU, an ancient name for God, I had asked my inner guide, the Mahanta,

220 PART THREE: SOUL TRAVEL

"Could I just see my father once more?" I had closed my eyes, relaxed, and opened an inner door, and there he was!

Did I visit him in his world or did he come to me? Was it via Soul Travel, the expansion of consciousness, or was it a dream? The only thing that mattered was that it was incredibly real. I had a conversation with my dad through the healing power of singing HU and the help of Divine Spirit.

At last I know—my father is alive and well in the heavens of God. I have felt his arms around me, been warmed by his love. Good-bye regrets, good-bye guilt. Love always finds a way.

54
The Kiss of God

Sally Thomas

*I*t all began at the kitchen sink. I was standing there washing the breakfast dishes, not expecting the spiritual experience to come.

Rays of early morning sun streamed across the backyard. As each beam of sunlight graced the lawn, it awakened a dormant dewdrop. In delicate fashion, the entire yard was transformed from a lush green carpet to an immense jewel box filled with multicolored, iridescent gems.

I paused in the middle of scrubbing a sudsy plate to enjoy the glistening scene. One dewdrop in particular caught my eye, a large blue bubble that gleamed with energy. Its vibrant distinction from the others was enchanting.

Suddenly, I was inside that translucent sphere in a world of bluish gray. Ahead stretched a long, narrow path leading into a hazy unknown. I began walking up that path, my dog, Shanti, by my side. After a few minutes we encountered a group of people gathered at the edge of a precipice.

Joining them, I recognized several people from my local area, a number of ECK Masters, and beings whom I did not know. At the feet of many sat a family pet. They had gathered to sing HU, a song of love and

221

gratitude that connects Soul to all of life. Softly, sweetly, the HU Song began. Each breath singing this prayer released the call of home, reflecting gratitude, exchanging love. As the sincerity of the singing increased, a fine spray descended upon the gathering—mist from the River of God.

It penetrated and cleansed, and cleansed again, until all that remained was purity. The HU continued, piercing, clear. The resonance transcended all belief.

Just when I thought I could bear no more, the force of the HU began to relent. With the fading of the melody, the spray gradually withdrew, returning to the River of God.

As the closing notes echoed in our hearts, a tiny blue sparkle flashed on top of each singer's head—a gift bestowed by God—like a kiss gently placed upon a baby's head.

With a start, I was back at the kitchen sink, hands immersed in soapy water. In the backyard, the large blue dewdrop gave a knowing twinkle and vanished.

I stood motionless, silently expressing thanks, then glanced down at the contented form of Shanti, stretched out on the kitchen floor, waiting for me to finish the dishes.

55

Two Ships in the Night

Niels-Jul Yrvin

One starry night I stood at the helm of a ship off the coast of Africa. About one o'clock in the morning I suddenly heard rain. The sky was cloudless. I went out to take a closer look. Peering over the side of the ship, I discovered several thousand dolphins jumping around in the water. Their splashing sounded like rain. In just a few minutes, as magically as they had appeared, they were gone, leaving me feeling blessed by the experience.

Sometime later, again on the ship's bridge, I was telling the chief steward my story of the dolphins, when we were alerted to a tanker on a collision course with us. She gave no sign of turning, as if she had not seen us. I hailed the ship on our radio.

On the VHF radio, the officer of the watch on the tanker advised me to stay on course. "I will turn starboard and sail around you," he said.

As I maintained our course, something strange happened. In my inner vision, I saw the bridge of the other ship and heard the officer give the order "Starboard 20 degrees."

Then I saw the helmsman turning the rudder the wrong way! I knew his mistake would result in a terrible accident if I did not react immediately. I quickly disconnected the automatic steering and put my helm hard to starboard.

Now I was in control of the situation. The other helmsman could do whatever he wanted, but he could not hit us.

The chief steward came running into the wheelhouse yelling, "He's turning the wrong way!"

I wasn't sure how to answer. Quietly I replied, "I have already turned the wheel. Whatever happens he cannot hit us."

He looked at me, astounded. "How could you know? I had the binoculars."

Again, I said quietly, "You know I have been sailing for many years. This is my job."

He left satisfied. No more questions were asked. I was relieved I didn't have to tell him how I had known what to do. I am sure he would not have believed me.

Telling the story of the dolphins must have opened my heart and made me more receptive to the conscious out-of-body experience that had saved our ship.

For me, Soul Travel has become a natural way to conduct my life from the viewpoint of Soul.

56

Soul Travel: A Touchstone Gift

Coleen Rehm

uddhism, Hinduism, Christianity, Taoism, Sufism, the teachings of Gurdjieff, Gandhi, Rampa, Krishnamurti—always another philosophy or teacher, and still never the entire truth. Pieces of this, fragments of that—my mind swirled in confusion. I closed the book and sighed, mildly frustrated, as I contemplated my imaginary "ideal spiritual path."

Maybe the key wasn't between the pages of any book. Maybe, just maybe, the truths of Divine Spirit were locked inside each Soul. In that moment I passionately wanted to know the truth of these spiritual matters.

So sudden was this rush of thoughts that the book slipped from my hand and tumbled to the floor. I sat transfixed, awestruck, as an inner voice chimed, "Trust."

Louder now, I heard it again, coupled with the distinct sensation that I was not alone. The room, even the very atmosphere, felt electrified with a new intensity, almost as if the universe paused in this moment, and waited. Yes, trust. Close the eyes and look within, contemplate. I was compelled by the very energy that permeated the room.

"Trust," chimed the inner voice. The feeling of

another presence was stronger now, almost as if I were being closely watched. Through my inner awareness, I sensed the importance of the moment. I trusted, and asked for God's protection in what I was about to do.

Solemnly, I lay comfortably on the floor and breathed deeply. Focusing my energy and attention on a point between my eyebrows, I sang a soft, lilting "HU-U-U," a word I'd read about in a teaching called Eckankar.

But after fifteen minutes, a minor distraction interrupted my concentration. It was the steady drip, drip, drip of a faucet. I sighed and got up to check all the faucets in the apartment, turning the hot and cold handles on every sink and tub. The sound was audible enough to fill every room I checked, but not one faucet was dripping. Puzzled, I returned to contemplation.

To my dismay, after only a few more minutes of singing "HU," I heard the dripping again! This time louder, more insistent, and faster.

Mildly exasperated, I once again made the rounds, checking all the plumbing, even under the sinks. The sound began to fade away as I checked the last sink. Dripless. Suddenly, with a start, I realized the sound had the same volume in every room I checked, whether there was a sink there or not. It seemed to follow me.

Listening more closely; I realized my inner being was laughing with an exhilaration that left me physically shaking. I heard the laughter; it was good-natured and tempered with wisdom.

"Trust," said the inner voice, "and go with it."

I smiled, lay back down on the carpet and eagerly began to chant HU again, eyes closed. Almost immediately, I heard the water dripping. The atoms of my being felt charged. Still, I sang HU. The sound became increasingly louder, as if all the taps in the house had been opened full force. Louder and louder, until it sounded as if I stood on the banks of Niagara Falls. Still I sang HU, and the HU blended with the roar of the water. I heard thunder off in the distance, and my being felt electrified.

I heard the sound of buzzing bees. Still, I kept my eyes closed, and sang HU, and trusted my inner voice, even as the buzzing overcame the water's roar, until the bees were all I heard.

Then the strangest sensation blanketed me. I heard the pop of a champagne cork flying from its bottle. Simultaneously, I felt and yet couldn't feel the carpet under my body. A sense of balance inside my head told me I was floating, moving slowly and surely upward. I gasped in astonishment. I could see myself lying on the floor, but my eyes were still closed.

I laughed, spinning and pirouetting in an ecstatic flight-dance. Then I shot as fast as I could from corner to corner, ceiling to floor, around the room. Giddily I floated in the uppermost corner and gazed at my body below. *Was I dead?* I wondered, noticing the luminous cord which connected me to the body I called myself. My inner awareness confirmed that my body was not dead, only resting for a while without me.

As I indulged in the luxury of my freedom, I wondered what the city looked like from this angle. Instantly I was on the roof outside, viewing a warm spring night filled with stars. Not one cloud marred the beauty of its moonless perfection.

"Would you like to continue onward?" asked a deep voice that was not my inner voice.

It was then that I became aware of the two spiritual guides. Their presence was not of light, nor sound, but a different, indescribable blending of both. "There may be a price to pay," the second guide joined in.

Suddenly I felt like a child learning to walk,

overexuberant in my joy at this newfound skill. I wanted to know all I could about these beings. Where had they come from and could they provide the answers to all the questions I'd ever had? I sensed a wise, almost paternal, caring in them as their energy touched and warmed me.

"Oh, yes," I said, "I want to know all that is."

I felt their presence grow, enfolding and surrounding me. Suddenly I could no longer see; darkness enveloped me. Trust, I remembered.

I sensed a rapidly moving elevator rising beneath us, scooping us up at hundreds of miles per hour, hurling us to the heavens. Faster and faster we traveled, and I heard the rush of wind louder than any hurricane or tornado. I felt our speed increasing as the wind turned to a giant droning hum. Then the hum dissolved into beautiful music, a symphony such as I'd never heard before. The music filled me with great happiness and sadness at the same time. In that moment I wanted to see, to experience fully the splendor of where I was. In that instant I felt the Light and was touched by the Sound.

The last strains of a melody I'll never fully remember and never completely forget lingered, finishing with the soft echo of a single note of a flute. I realized I was again in the uppermost corner of my room, floating with the Beings of Light and Sound. Possibly I'd been there all along.

I felt myself becoming imperceptibly heavier. "Don't go," I begged. "Or, at least, come back sometime. Teach me more."

"The teacher will come when the student is ready," said one.

"But when? I'm ready now," I entreated them. I felt myself drifting inexorably toward my body.

"Soon," said the first voice. "Develop patience."

"But how will I know?" I recalled my frantic search over the past ten years through so many philosophies and teachings, leading me to this moment.

"You will know. Trust your inner knowingness." Then slowly, I rocked back into my body, and they were gone, leaving a glow in the air and on my cheeks.

They were right. I met the teacher on this earthly plane about six months later. Yes, they were right about my recognizing him. It must have been the subtle blue glow (at first glance) that danced about his head and shoulders.

That was years ago. Daily, I thank the Inner Master, the Mahanta, for that spiritual experience with the Light and Sound; a touchstone gift from God.

57

Was It Just My Imagination?

Laura Reave

I had been a member of Eckankar for several years before I had an opportunity to teach a class. The current topic involved Soul Travel. The group agreed to try an imaginative technique at home, write down the results, and report back at our next meeting. Several very adept Soul Travelers were in the class, and I was looking forward to hearing about some great experiences the next time we met.

There was just one little problem: since I was the teacher of the class, I had to participate. I had always felt that I didn't have a very good imagination.

I had been fortunate to have plenty of experience with the Light and Sound of God through my spiritual exercises. But when it came to imagining conversations with ECK Masters or visits to spiritual temples, I either drew a blank or felt that whatever I imagined was just a fantasy.

I knew I had to sit myself down and do my assignment, so I could at least say I gave it a try. I began by singing HU, an ancient name for God.

"HU-U-U-U," I sang, then I began instructing myself through the exercise. "OK, now imagine you're walking down a path, and you see a temple up ahead." Nothing. "OK, so an ECK Master comes up to greet you, and he says, 'Welcome to the temple of . . .'" Nothing.

Well, I thought, *maybe I'll try the 'as if' principle—I'll act as if I could actually do this exercise.* If I could actually do this exercise, this is where I would go and this is what I would do.

So I began to tell myself a story about a woman named Laura who went to a temple with very high ceilings and polished marble floors. I went to an alcove where the Shariyat-Ki-Sugmad, the holy scriptures of ECK, stood alone, shining brightly, and I read a sentence or two.

I ended my exercise quickly, so I could remember as much as possible to write down. There. At least now I would have something to bring to class.

True to form, some of the members of the class had incredible experiences. I gave a brief report, saying I wasn't sure if it happened or not. Relieved that the project was over, I gladly returned to my regular spiritual exercises and left imaginative exercises to those with imagination.

Months later at a friend's house, I was getting dressed to go swimming. I noticed some pictures on the wall. They were sketches of Temples of Golden Wisdom drawn by an ECK initiate. *How fascinating,* I thought. *That someone could actually see the temples well enough to draw . . .*

I was struck dumb. My whole body felt the shock of recognition when I came to the picture in the center, a temple with high ceilings and polished marble floors, and I heard myself say, "I was *there!*"

He said nothing, yet his message of welcome and love was quite clear. I was accepted, I was released, I was loved.

58

Isn't There More to Life?

Bo Coyle

*I*f material things really mattered, I had it all. A great job, a loving wife and beautiful daughters, a house on the golf course, and a Mercedes in the garage. Quiet, comfortable, and well into the American dream, nevertheless I felt like a child on Christmas morning who looks at all his gifts and says, "Is this all there is?"

Over the months, the nagging emptiness grew into an ache. An important part of my life was missing. My successful little world was becoming meaningless in the face of a growing longing I couldn't understand. Then early one cold morning while I was out running, I had a sudden realization. I stopped and looked up at the stars in a dark sky.

What I am missing isn't here on earth! I thought. My heart yearned for something in the heavens.

Grief engulfed me, as I realized this made me a prisoner of life. The tears froze on my cheeks as my silent cry went out into the dark sky: "Please, please, bring me home."

Better sense returned as I finished my run. No matter what I felt, my responsibilities were still unchanged.

Soon a warm shower relaxed my inner turmoil, and

I tried an imaginative technique to clear out some of the unhappiness that haunted me. I visualized traveling back up the stream of hot water, all the way to its source deep in the well in the backyard. Suddenly the darkness turned into a light that burned into my eyes. As I adjusted to the brightness, beautiful music welled up. It sounded like hundreds of voices singing. A man in a white robe came out of this intoxicating light and sound. He reached out his arms in welcome.

I looked into his eyes. The love was almost too much to bear. For the first time in my life I knew I was home.

He said nothing, yet his message of welcome and love was quite clear. I was accepted, I was released, I was loved.

The experience ended as quickly as it began. The next thing I knew, I was on my knees in the shower—weeping for the second time that day! This time I cried in wonder and longing. There was a place for me! All I had to do was find it.

During the next few days, the idea of going to the public library kept popping into my mind. Finally I decided to go look for a book to tell me what had happened.

I was determined to know who the man was and how I could get back to the love and light.

As I browsed the library's religious and metaphysical sections, I caught a glimpse of someone in white in the next aisle. My attention shifted back to the titles, as a movement from above caught my eye. A blue book was being pushed off the shelf from the other side.

I caught the small paperback just before it hit me and called out to the person on the other side, "Hey!"

There was no answer. I stormed around the rack, blue book in hand, to see who was there. Did they know what they had done? There was no one there. Not a soul was standing anywhere near.

I went back to return the blue book and resume my search. But as I lifted it up, the title caught my eye: *The Spiritual Notebook* by Paul Twitchell, the modern-day founder of Eckankar. I thumbed through the pages, stopping every once in a while to read paragraphs that seemed to jump out at me. It was as if this book had been written just for me!

Here were answers to questions that had bothered me for years. Past experiences began to make sense. Here too were spiritual exercises to help me in my quest to return "home."

The day that blue book fell into my hands was a turning point in my life. It was the day I found Eckankar and my personal path home to God.

59

A Lesson from the Masters

Jim Hawkins

Throughout the writings of Eckankar, there are listed literally hundreds of spiritual exercises that the student of Divine Spirit can try in order to reach spiritual liberation.

One spiritual exercise that fascinated me was mentioned by Paul Twitchell, the modern-day founder of Eckankar. In this spiritual exercise, one sits comfortably in a chair, and while the eyes are closed, places his attention on the Tisra Til, the Spiritual Eye, and softly chants the word *HU* to himself while visualizing the face of one of the ECK Masters on the blank screen of the mind.

I had been reading the fascinating biography of the great ECK saint Milarepa and tried this technique for several days without any success. Then, on the fourth day, when my mind gave up on its almost obsessive desire to have an experience with this particular Master, I fell asleep (or, at least, I think I did), and had the following experience:

The mountain air was crisp and cold as I walked along the rugged mountain trail. I wondered where I was, and instantly the knowledge came to me that this was the Hindu Kush mountain range in Afghanistan and Pakistan, home base of the ECK Master Rebazar

Tarzs. But I was not to meet Rebazar Tarzs tonight. As I rounded a sharp bend in the trail, I came upon a monk in a clean brown robe. His face was kind and ageless, and his eyes had a sparkle that I have seen in few men. Before I could even greet him, he said, "So, you wish to meet Milarepa? Well, here I am. What is it you want?"

I must admit I was rather dumbfounded by the whole experience, and before I could think I said, "I want an experience I will never forget." (I have since learned that one should be a little more specific, especially when dealing with an ECK Master.)

Milarepa chuckled to himself, and the next thing I knew another monk rounded the corner with a large stick in his hand.

"Oh no, Marpa," Milarepa said to the small, determined-looking man. "I am sure you won't need to use that on him."

"I guess you're right," he said to Milarepa, putting down the stick, much to my relief. "You there, you want an experience? Remember what you asked for. Now come with me, and be quick about it!"

The next thing I knew, Marpa had jogging shoes on and was running up the trail. "If you want your experience, you had better catch up with him," Milarepa said. I really hate running, but I knew I had to follow Marpa or my experience would be for naught. I ran as fast as I could, but only managed to stay just behind him as we journeyed up to the mountain peak.

Exhausted, I collapsed at his feet. Marpa looked at me and snarled, "Stand up! There is something I must show you."

I stood up, and he pointed his wrinkled finger to a valley below the mountain. "Do you see that valley?" "Yes," I managed to reply. "There is a stone quarry down there. You will run down the mountain, bring up as many stones as you can carry, and build a foundation on this spot where we are standing. When you think you are finished, I will examine your foundation to see if it is sturdy enough to support the house you are going to build on it. Now get moving!" Marpa commanded.

After countless trips up and down the mountain, carrying heavy loads of rocks to the top, I was finally finished building my foundation. I stood on top of it, bruised and bleeding, but with a wonderful sense of accomplishment. Much to my surprise, Sri Harold Klemp, the Mahanta, the Living ECK Master came walking up the trail, accompanied by Milarepa.

"Well, Jim, I see you met Marpa," he said, grinning at me. "Milarepa and I have had to build and rebuild several houses. Each new one better than the last. Come, let me show you something."

I followed Sri Harold down the mountain to a large valley and saw an enormously large foundation that Marpa, Milarepa, and countless others were working on.

Marpa then strode up to me and said, "When you are finished with your foundation, you can join us in working on this one!" A wide grin crossed his face, and Milarepa laughed heartily in the background as Marpa walked back to resume his work.

Sri Harold looked at me and said in a humorous vein, "Well, I guess that says it all."

With those words still ringing in my ear, I came out of my contemplation, exhausted, yet full of vitality. The only question that came to my mind was, Yes, when are we going to finish building our own foundations, so we can help the ECK Masters with the one they are building?

An interesting question, don't you think?

60

Saved by Out-of-Body Travel

Ken Uzzell

*I*t was a wintry night, and I was driving my new motorbike through a national park. Rounding a curve, I misjudged the turn and slammed the bike into the rocky overhang. The impact flung me over the handlebar and head-on into a telegraph pole.

Instantly, I found myself thirty feet above the wreckage, wondering who owned that broken body below. The feeling was similar to dreams from my youth. It then dawned on me—I was out of my body!

As I hovered there in a new, shining body, wondering what would become of me, a powerful voice entered my being. It offered a choice between crossing the borders into the unknown or returning to my physical body. There was so much love, power, and wisdom pouring from this wonderful being, it was frightening.

With some difficulty, the shining being that was me aligned itself with the physical body on the ground. I couldn't get back into the physical body fast enough and snapped awake with a full realization of what had just occurred.

The national park was closed to traffic, so I faced a ten-kilometer walk to safety. After a few hundred yards, the pain, internal bleeding, and broken bones caused me to black out.

When I came to, I was lying in the middle of the road, the winter wind and rain chilling me to the bone. Slowly I opened my eyes and looked at the dark sky, saying to an invisible God, "Well, if you want me to live, how about a hand? I can't go on."

Then something special happened. The rain stopped, the wind died, and the clouds parted to reveal a full moon. All was silent. The pain ebbed as I was encircled in a ball of white light and lifted to my feet. I found myself drifting along the road—not conscious of walking at all.

After a short time, I came to the gates of the park, where the lights of a car snapped me back to reality. Some kind strangers put me in the back of their car and drove to the hospital.

When I told the nurses and doctors of this wonderful experience, they thought I was hallucinating and insisted that I couldn't have walked ten feet—let alone ten kilometers. Later that night, an orthopedic surgeon listened as I repeated the story. He displayed little reaction, but when he returned the next morning, he was obviously in shock.

I had explained how I picked up my motorbike helmet at the beginning of my walk. Later, when the car appeared, I discarded it. The surgeon had driven out to the scene of the accident and measured the distance between the smashed motorbike and the helmet, which he found beside the road.

He stood at my bedside telling me that I had walked ten kilometers in under an hour—an impossible feat, considering the injuries I had sustained!

* * *

Five years later, while attending my first Eckankar seminar, I had the opportunity to meet and speak with the Living ECK Master. When I heard his voice, I recognized it immediately. It was the voice of the being who had spoken to me the night of the accident.

61

A Soul Travel Visit
to the Other Worlds

Robert Scott Rochek

had a Soul Travel experience at the 1986 Eckankar International Creative Arts Festival in New Orleans. As an ECKist, I know that the Mahanta's presence is always with me. But it's still up to me to go beyond the small, physical state of consciousness and allow the God-self to unfold within me.

I was attending a workshop on how to visit the Temples of Golden Wisdom on the inner spiritual planes. As we were led through a visualization technique, I consciously met Wah Z and Tibetan ECK Master Rebazar Tarzs near the Temple of Golden Wisdom in the city of Retz on Venus.

The Soul Travel experience began with a faint scent of sandalwood. Suddenly I was standing on a white-marble path surrounded by beautiful flowers. As I glanced to the left, I saw a gold light laced with glowing violet. Wah Z was there, and he introduced me to Rebazar Tarzs. The Tibetan ECK Master looked penetratingly into my eyes and said, "Now your true journey into the worlds of God shall begin. Will you submit to my guidance and do as I say?"

"Yes, Sri Tarzs, I will!"

"Will you abide by the word of the Mahanta?" he asked.

I turned to Wah Z and said, "Yes, Mahanta, I will!"

Then Wah Z told me to step into the swirling light. As I did this, the brilliant gold-and-violet light spiraled up and around and through me, penetrating every cell.

"Now you are filled with the Light and Sound of ECK," declared Rebazar. "All will be well with you!" He led me up the steps of marble into the Temple of Golden Wisdom.

Wah Z was by my side as I entered a small room to the right of the main chamber. It was brilliantly lit from within by golden-white light. As I moved toward the light, I saw a rectangular marble pedestal about two feet wide and three feet high. Atop it rested a transparent glasslike container, filled with glowing script in an unknown tongue. It seemed as if one could read from this form of the Shariyat-Ki-Sugmad, the holy scriptures of Eckankar, via energy imprints of Light and Sound.

On closer inspection, the writing seemed to be moving—alive and changing within the box, which was filled with a fluid, viscous substance. Telepathically, Wah Z told me that this Shariyat wasn't read like words on a page. Rather, one simply touched the box with one's hands, and waves of Spirit-filled Sound and Light were transmitted directly into the chela. This was a most astounding realization to me!

Meanwhile in the physical body, I was sitting in the workshop writing furiously, with one eye on the inner and the other on the page before me. As I placed my hands on the Shariyat-Ki-Sugmad, this is what was transmitted, as I experienced and recorded it:

"The Shariyat-Ki-Sugmad is the condensed Sound and Light of ECK in a form that is tangible and can be understood by beings while in the inner planes. It is the actual wisdom of Sugmad (God), that part of the vibrations of ECK which that particular section of the Shariyat represents. This is why one can touch one of these forms of the Shariyat and have the vibration, or wisdom, of that particular Shariyat transmitted directly into him—Sound and Light being what the Shariyat really is."

But the most important part of this Soul Travel experience came after I returned again to the workshop.

The speaker asked if any were willing to share their inner journeys. At first I was hesitant, but the Mahanta let me know that it would be for the greatest good to tell others, and I did. As I stood to speak, the students nearest me passed a microphone, so all could hear. I realized that they had accompanied me to the pedestal of the Shariyat. Now they were eager to hear of my experience and confirm their own inner journeys.

As I read the message given me, many faces lit up. I felt we were joined together on this path of the Golden Heart.

After the workshop a young man came up to me with his eyes agleam. He had often visited this same wisdom temple but had been frustrated in his attempts to read the living Shariyat as if it were an ordinary book. Because I had been allowed to help others learn, I experienced such gratitude and love from this Soul. He had finally learned the secret of placing his hands on the surface of the Shariyat, so now the ECK within it could flow to him via the Golden Heart. He gained something he'd wanted for a long time, and by being a channel for ECK, I gained more than words can ever express.

I was shown how the greater experiences of spiritual worth come from giving—not from the little self, which continually demands to receive. I look forward to each moment in the nowness of eternity with the Mahanta, as I unfold in conscious awareness of Divine Spirit and the God-self within me.

62
A Good-bye to Grandma

Coleen Rehm

*T*remember my mother's letter, the one that
came right after Thanksgiving, telling me that
Grandma had broken her hip.

"Write and send cards, but don't mention anything
about a nursing home," my mother wrote. "We plan to
get her back into her apartment as soon as possible."

As I read her words, I envisioned my grandmother
miles away and lost in a sea of hospital white. A wave
of memories rose and crested over me as I recalled
Grandma's great love.

I remember her quiet knowingness. She was the
first person who could gaze at me and, without words,
convey a deep understanding of my true inner being.

She would always tell children how special they
were to her and how she loved them. She praised each
talent and fostered awareness of each individual's
accomplishments. And when she planted a kiss on your
forehead, it was a stamp of pride and measureless love.

I remember the weekends I spent with Grandma
when I was sixteen. We'd sit for hours, knitting and
crocheting and talking of many things: her childhood,
the changing century, God, morality in the modern
world, and the meaning of life. Always Grandma would
weigh each question (no matter how controversial) and

offer one carefully balanced opinion. And always, she would conclude with, "Remember, I love you, no matter what." Then she'd laugh, a half chuckle ending in a half sigh, and clasp my hand in her warm, finely blue-veined hand. I can still see how clearly her eyes sparkled like diamonds in those moments.

I grew up and left home, but I kept my grandmother close, always in my heart. And when the letters could not fill the distance, I'd call or fly in for the weekend.

I remember one weekend shortly after the doctor's diagnosis that Grandma had cancer. Amid cancer-therapy treatments, I flew in.

I had a light lunch with her and afterward offered to wash the dishes. As I finished drying the last plate and turned from the sink, I saw Grandma from the corner of my eye as she inadvertently caught her foot between the chair legs and stumbled.

Face distraught, she seized the table edge with one delicately blue-veined hand and impatiently waved away the near accident, blaming a scattered throw rug. Beyond the surface of her frayed emotions, I saw reflections of fear and pain.

I could barely glimpse the familiar blue sparkle in her eyes. "How about a hug from my sweet Grandma?" I asked softly.

In a rush, she clung to me: a frail embrace, tempered by uncertainty. Silently, I chanted HU-U-U-U, declaring myself an open channel for the ECK, in the name of the Mahanta. I felt a warm glow of love enveloping us, and the tremor of a chill passed up my spine.

Motionless, we held each other close. I felt an orange light swirl about our bodies, the transforming and diffusing purity of the Light and Sound of God.

Gradually, I felt her calm in my arms. Gently she

took my face in her hands, her blue eyes again sparkling like diamonds. She laughed that funny little half chuckle, half sigh, smiled, and kissed my cheek. *Thank you, Mahanta,* I mused inwardly. I knew in that moment, that everything would be all right.

Grandma recovered from the treatments, as well as the cancer, and for that she was most grateful. We never mentioned that moment in the kitchen, but on an unspoken level, we knew we had grown even closer.

Like a stream that flows simultaneously on many levels in many directions, the ECK was moving in our lives. With those simple words in my mother's letter, "don't mention anything about a nursing home," I had inwardly decided to relocate to care for my Grandma.

In a matter of weeks, the wheels were set in motion. Having given notice at my job and apartment, it seemed nothing could stop me from moving near Grandma. But, with only two weeks left to go, I found myself inexplicably caught in a state of half-packed and half-yet-to-be-packed. A restless, aimless feeling in me suggested there was something I had neglected to recognize, something I needed to do. This mood overrode my whirlwind of plans and brought me to a standstill. My mind was 350 miles away with my Grandma, and I was eager to be with her. Maybe if I called, she might be awake.

"No, no, Aunt Janet, don't wake her, OK? But would you do me a favor? Just tell her I love her. I know she knows, but would you tell her as soon as she wakes up? Thanks, and I love you too."

The aching longingness to be with my Grandma grew more insistent. I had to be with her *NOW.* A sudden knowingness crystallized within me.

"Mahanta, be with me," I murmured. I sat down, closed my eyes, and Soul Traveled to see her.

She was sleeping in the upstairs bedroom in Aunt Janet's colonial home. Her walker stood like a sentinel between the twin beds. Grandma curled softly on her side in the left bed, the flowing bedspread rising and falling with each breath.

Grandma, Grandma! I love you, Grandma. Can you hear me? I wondered in my thoughts.

"Oh yes, darlin', just fine, but where are you?"

"Right here, Grandma. Right here, in your dreams."

In her sleep, she gently rolled on her back, one arm flung around her head. I held her hand.

"And I love you too, sweetheart."

I felt a flow of love pass in waves between us, bathing us in a warm and tangible glow. The presence of the Mahanta was a Blue Light in the upper corner of the room. "How are you, Grandma?"

"Just fine." I sensed by her inflection that this was a rote response.

"No, Grandma. How are you *really* feeling?"

"Well, sweetheart, when one gets to be so old, little aches and pains appear; and we simply learn to adjust and gradually grow accustomed to them in our lives. Like this broken hip." She chuckled to herself, but her humor ended in a sigh. "So we do what we must, once the body begins to wear out, gets old. Sometimes I ache so, missing your Grandpa." She began to ramble in her memories.

"You loved him very much, didn't you?"

"Why, yes, I did. It's been quite lonely at times, without him. He was always such a comfort to me. Though if one of us should have to go sooner, it was easier for me to go on alone than it would have been for your Grandpa."

"You know I love you, Grandma, but you know you

can go if you want to."

"Well now, sweetheart, what about your plans? You've given notice on your little apartment and your job so you could move down. What would happen if there were a change in plans?"

"I'll be all right."

"If I went, how would the rest of the family be?"

"Just fine, Grandma. I know you've missed Grandpa a lot these past ten years. Would you like to see him? You can."

"See Jack again? I have missed him so." Her voice broke in a question, "How can I see him?" I sensed the Blue Light of the Mahanta expanding and filling the room behind me. Reaching to smooth my grandmother's hair, I felt support and strength in the presence of the Master.

"This is a friend of mine, Grandma. He is the Mahanta. Whenever you want, he'll take you to Grandpa. You just decide when." I felt the love of the Master envelop and fill the three of us. *Please take good care of her, Mahanta,* I thought.

"What a pretty blue light around your friend, Mahanta. I've always liked blue, you know," Grandma mused quietly. Her face shone at the thought of seeing Grandpa. "I've always wanted to go suddenly, without pain," she said. "Yes, unexpectedly, while doing some daily little activity, like taking my medication. Yes, that would be nice; and oh, to see Jack again." A tear rolled down her cheek and soaked into the pillowcase. Gently squeezing her hand, I said, "I love you, Grandma."

"And I love you too, Sweetheart."

"Thank you, Mahanta."

The tremorous sigh was my own. I covered my face with my hands and suddenly felt very human, very fragile. My grandmother had passed on.

Outside my window is a slim dark-limbed tree. On rainy spring nights, it catches the cool rain. And when the streetlights shine, it sparkles like diamonds, reminding me of Grandma.

63

Suicide, Recovery, and Revelation

Ellen Adams

I was raised and married in a very strict religion. This religion taught that you married for life. But after a few months of marriage, my husband started seeing other women.

Thinking there was no way out, I placed a gun over my heart and pulled the trigger. The gun kicked as I fired, and I missed my heart by about a quarter of an inch. I lay on the floor for five and a half hours, slipping in and out of consciousness. Then my husband found me, and the next thing I remembered was one of the medics crying over me in the ambulance because I was dying.

I took his hand and patted it—his tears seemed so sweet and silly. I'd had so many problems and had not wanted to live. Besides, he didn't even know me! But my hand went right through his.

I realized with shock that I was out of my physical body. I was only patting him with my Astral, or Light, body.

This condition of being separated from the body continued as we moved into an operating room. I thought, *Well, this is what the preacher was preaching about, when he said we don't stay in our body at death.* But it still hadn't quite hit me that the body on the operating table was mine. I floated up to where the nurses and residents were watching my operation. *I hope that little girl makes it,* I thought, gazing down compassionately.

Slowly I floated back down and realized with a shock that it really was me on that table! In a rush, I tried to leave the operating room. But some kindly spiritual beings rounded me up and took me to a higher place where the earthly scene faded.

We progressed along a winding brick corridor, where I met the Angel of Death. He transferred this thought to me: *We're going to go back through your life and review what's happened so far.* This scared me, because I'd been raised not to believe in some Grim Reaper. We started reviewing my life from babyhood forward. When we reached an image of me at age four, a sound completely interrupted the review. *HU-U-U-U.*

Suddenly I was enveloped in brilliant white light and escorted out of the room. That sound had saved me from the Angel of Death.

It was like a thousand people singing *HU-U-U-U.* Then right before I reentered my body, my heart was impressed with a single word: *Sugmad.* Remember, I'd never heard of Eckankar. Since then I've learned that Sugmad is an Eckankar term for God and that HU, pronounced like *hue,* is a holy name of God sung for upliftment.

As I grasped the word *Sugmad,* I said to myself, "I've got to remember this; I've got to remember this." The next thing I knew, I was coming out of a two-week coma. I couldn't walk or talk, and I had a long way to go in rehabilitation.

But I wasn't unhappy. On the contrary, for the first

time I understood a little about why I'd wanted to die. Somehow I knew that I had lived before, and I'd been a female ruler in Iran. I'd had seven advisers who often acted without my authority, because they disregarded women in that culture. They even took people's lives in my name. My sin, if you will, was that I didn't express my authority and what I knew. I ended that life in suicide. So my karma, the effects of my actions, from that life was again acted out, complete with deep anguish. My husband had been one of my strongest advisers in that life.

It took me a lot of work to get back into this life. But events unfolded in a much happier way. I was now on a search for truth. I divorced my husband, and two years later, I found the Eckankar teachings. I was visiting a girlfriend and remarked on a picture of Sri Harold Klemp, the Mahanta, the Living ECK Master that she had in her home. She gave me a book to read on this religion, which was new to me. I thumbed through and left the book at home while I went on vacation.

On the first night of my return, I read a little further. Later that night, a blue light appeared outside my bedroom window. "Oh no!" I said. "I'm going crazy." I thrust my head under the bedcovers. But I could still see this light—even from under the covers!

The light filled my room. I hadn't read anything about the blue light yet, that it can be a sign of the presence of the Mahanta. A voice emanated from the light: "Go to Michie, call Michie." (Michie was my friend in Eckankar). I did, and eventually I became a member of ECK. Over my years of study, I've also learned more about the two words I'd heard while in my coma: *HU* and *Sugmad*.

Now my viewpoint on life is completely different.

Before the Mahanta showed his love for me in these profound ways, I couldn't understand anything about my misery and just wanted to end it all. Now I wouldn't dare pass up the gift of this life! I know it is a precious opportunity to grow and learn. I'm now happily living a new life under the guidance of the Mahanta, Sri Harold Klemp.

Moving about the battlefield were other Souls from many different faiths, working, like myself, with strength and compassion.

64

My Spiritual Tour of Duty

Walt Wrzesniewski

The day after the United Nations' deadline for Iraq's withdrawal from Kuwait, my wife and I sat down to supper in the United States. Suddenly I felt as if I were surrounded by exploding bombs. I could feel the terrific concussions and hear the explosions. I could see the dirt fly up. As Soul, I observed this with a dispassionate, yet compassionate, spiritual vision, feeling no pain or fear.

I turned my attention back to my wife, still sitting at our tranquil supper table, and announced that the bombing had just started. The war in the Persian Gulf had begun. A short time later the television newscasters confirmed this.

Over the next few months in my thoughts, dreams, and contemplations, I spent much time Soul Traveling throughout the Middle East. This was my spiritual tour of duty.

One morning I awoke and told my wife that Saddam Hussein was hidden in a bunker below his presidential palace. I knew he was unafraid, even calm in the midst of the chaos of war. In time, television broadcasts would confirm this.

One day I found my attention on a battlefield. The bodies of Iraqi soldiers were scattered about. Some

Souls lingered near their lifeless physical bodies, not quite sure what they should do. Other Souls swayed, drifting almost completely out of the body then back inside again. The rest of the soldiers were in great shock and pain, but here and there some felt relief.

I was not alone in my spiritual mission. Moving about the battlefield were other Souls from many different faiths, working, like myself, with strength and compassion.

We were all working together with the purest love to help the soldiers. Some of the soldiers were guided across the veil of death, some were given strength to handle pain, and some found the comfort they needed to regain their composure.

Once, in my inner travels, I came upon a mother and her young son hiding under a stairway. She enveloped her child in her arms as the nearby bombing filled the air with dust. Backed into a corner, she prayed fiercely for help. These prayers were answered. Although the bombing continued, she felt the comfort and knew the serenity of the Light and Sound of God.

Battlefield duty was only a small part of the spiritual service for which we were commissioned during the war in the Persian Gulf. We guided downed airmen and pointed the way for the rescuers searching for them. We reached out to comfort families and other loved ones when news of a loss arrived. And we helped lighten the fears of those people who huddled in desperation while the world shook terribly around them.

Throughout these experiences, I was filled with gratitude to the Mahanta, the Living ECK Master that I could be of help in this way. Serving God is the highest duty, and duty was never so gratifying.

65

One Easy Lesson

Doug Munson

One weekend, not too long ago, in the early spring I was home alone. My wife, April, and our two boys were spending the weekend with her mother so I could finish painting the house without interruption.

By Saturday night I was exhausted after running up and down the extension ladder and waving a paint-brush around with my right hand. I fixed a sandwich and plunked myself down in front of the TV for a few minutes to eat my supper. Then I shut off the television and got ready for bed without even bothering to take care of my plate in the living room.

In the middle of the night, as stars twinkled and crickets chirped outside, I suddenly sensed a presence in the bedroom. With a start I realized my nine-year-old son was standing at the foot of the bed. He was in his underwear, with his hands on his hips.

"Dad," he said, "you didn't put your dishes away." He stepped briskly out of the bedroom into the hallway.

I shouted in surprise, "How did you get here? You're supposed to be with your mother."

"Oh, I just missed you and wanted to say hi."

I ran after him down the hall. He was already down the stairs leading to the front door.

"I have to go back and be with Mom now. I love you."
And off he went. As I stood at the top of the stairs, I
was struck with the realization that I was out of my
body.

"This is too real to be a dream," I said to myself.
I walked past the plate on the living-room floor, into
the kitchen. The house was strangely lit. There were
no lights on, but I could clearly see where I was going.

Boy, I could go anywhere, I thought. *I could explore
the universe. I could ask the Inner Master to visit.*

But I turned and walked back down the hallway.
Curiosity gripped me. Slowly I inched my way back to
the bedroom, anxious about what I would see when I
stepped through the door.

"Son of a gun. There I am," I said out loud. A wave
of love rolled through my heart for that reclining, snoring
temple under the covers. "It's all true. Proof positive.
I am Soul."

As I moved closer to the bed, I heard a high-pitched
humming. It grew louder and louder. In an instant I
was back in my body, swatting at the mosquito buzzing
in my ear. I jolted awake with my mouth open, knowing
I was not the same person who had crawled into bed
earlier that night.

For some, the thought of being out of the body may
not be exactly reassuring. For those on the path of
Eckankar, it can become a way of life. In a very real
way, the Mahanta, the Living ECK Master had given
me one easy lesson about Soul, about how to walk the
path to Self-Realization and God-Realization.

66

A Spiritual Exercise to Try

Harold Klemp

When you step onto the path to God and you begin looking for that secret path to heaven, the way will be opened for you. And the way lies through the Spiritual Exercises of ECK.

These spiritual exercises link you with the guidance of the Holy Spirit, which is seen as Light and heard as Sound. The inner Sound is the Voice of God calling us home. The inner Light is a beacon to light our way. All the Spiritual Exercises of ECK are built on these two divine aspects of the Holy Spirit.

When you do the Spiritual Exercises of ECK, fill yourself with love and goodwill. Do one exercise every day. Spend about twenty minutes on it. This builds your spiritual stamina gently over time. Regular daily practice is the key to success. This exercise is from my book *The Spiritual Exercises of ECK*.

Dreams, Soul Travel, and Love

There are many ECK spiritual exercises. Each one opens you a little bit more to the Sound and Light of God.

This spiritual exercise is for three different groups of people: (1) those who don't dream but want to, (2) those who dream but want to Soul Travel, and

(3) those who want to go beyond dreams and Soul Travel to the state of direct knowingness. The exercise is so simple that it may seem as if I'm belittling your intelligence, but I'm not. Truth is always simple.

Just before you go to sleep, sit quietly on your bed. Close your eyes. Chant HU (pronounced *hue*) very softly, or if someone is in the room with you, chant it silently to yourself. HU is a special word, the ancient name for God. You could call it the manifested Word or the Sound; it has a power of its own.

As you take the time to sit there and chant HU, the name of God, you are making a commitment with Divine Spirit. Chant HU in a long, drawn-out way for three or four or five minutes, and let yourself settle down. Then wait for a few more minutes before starting the next step.

For those who have been unable to remember their dreams, simply chant the word *dream* spelled out. Chant it out loud, letter by letter: D-R-E-A-M. Do this for about five minutes. Next, chant the same thing quietly for a few minutes, and then just go to sleep. As you are falling asleep, say, "I would like to remember a significant spiritual dream." With this method, you are asking for truth to come through the dream state.

Some of you want Soul Travel, which is usually an advanced state beyond the dream state. Again, sit on your bed or on the floor, shut your eyes, and look into your Spiritual Eye. This is located at a point just above and between the eyebrows. Don't expect to see anything there; just chant HU, the holy name of God.

Then spell out *Soul Travel,* chanting each separate letter: S-O-U-L T-R-A-V-E-L. Do this about three times out loud and then three times quietly.

Those who have Soul Traveled may now want to go to the higher state of direct knowingness, without having to go through the intermediary stages. Dreams and Soul Travel are helpful and important, but at some point you outgrow them.

Simply chant the words *divine love.* Originally I was going to give it as L-O-V-E, but some people would mix it up with human love. The word *divine* takes it beyond human love. Divine love brings you all forms of love, including human love. To limit it to the usual definition of love is like working from the bottom, instead of working from the top of spirituality.

So, chant D-I-V-I-N-E L-O-V-E. This means you seek the highest form of love, which brings all blessings to you.

Glossary

Words set in SMALL CAPS are defined elsewhere in this glossary.

BLUE LIGHT. How the MAHANTA often appears in the inner worlds to the CHELA or seeker.

CHELA. *CHEE-lah* A spiritual student. Often refers to a member of ECKANKAR.

ECK. *EHK* The Life Force, the Holy Spirit, or Audible Life Current which sustains all life.

ECKANKAR. *EHK-ahn-kahr* Religion of the Light and Sound of God. Also known as the Ancient Science of SOUL TRAVEL. A truly spiritual religion for the individual in modern times. The teachings provide a framework for anyone to explore their own spiritual experiences. Established by PAUL TWITCHELL, the modern-day founder, in 1965. The word means "Co-worker with God."

ECK MASTER(S). Spiritual Masters who can assist and protect people in their spiritual studies and travels. The ECK Masters are from a long line of God-Realized SOULS who know the responsibility that goes with spiritual freedom.

FUBBI QUANTZ. *FOO-bee KWAHNTS* The guardian of the SHARIYAT-KI-SUGMAD at the Katsupari Monastery in northern Tibet. He was the MAHANTA, the LIVING ECK MASTER during the time of Buddha, about 500 BC.

GOD-REALIZATION. The state of God Consciousness. Complete and conscious awareness of God.

GOPAL DAS. *GOH-pahl DAHS* The guardian of the SHARIYAT-KI-SUGMAD at the Temple of Askleposis on the Astral PLANE. He was the MAHANTA, the LIVING ECK MASTER in Egypt, about 3,000 BC.

HU. *HYOO* The most ancient, secret name for God. The singing of the word *HU* is considered a love song to God. It can be sung aloud or silently to oneself.

271

INITIATION. Earned by a member of ECKANKAR through spiritual unfoldment and service to God. The initiation is a private ceremony in which the individual is linked to the Sound and Light of God.

KARMA, LAW OF. The Law of Cause and Effect, action and reaction, justice, retribution, and reward, which applies to the lower or psychic worlds: the Physical, Astral, Causal, Mental, and Etheric Planes

KLEMP, HAROLD. The present MAHANTA, the LIVING ECK MASTER. SRI Harold Klemp became the Mahanta, the Living ECK Master in 1981. His spiritual name is WAH Z.

LAI TSI. *lie TSEE* An ancient Chinese ECK MASTER.

LIVING ECK MASTER. The title of the spiritual leader of ECKANKAR. His duty is to lead SOUL back to God. The Living ECK Master can assist spiritual students physically as the Outer Master, in the dream state as the Dream Master, and in the spiritual worlds as the Inner Master.

MAHANTA. *mah-HAHN-tah* A title to describe the highest state of God Consciousness on earth, often embodied in the LIVING ECK MASTER. He is the Living Word. An expression of the Spirit of God that is always with you.

PLANE(S). The levels of existence, such as the Physical, Astral, Causal, Mental, Etheric, and SOUL Planes.

REBAZAR TARZS. *REE-bah-zahr TAHRZ* A Tibetan ECK MASTER known as the torchbearer of ECKANKAR in the lower worlds.

SATSANG. *SAHT-sahng* A class in which students of ECK study a monthly lesson from ECKANKAR.

SELF-REALIZATION. SOUL recognition. The entering of Soul into the Soul PLANE and there beholding Itself as pure Spirit. A state of seeing, knowing, and being.

SHARIYAT-KI-SUGMAD. *SHAH-ree-aht-kee-SOOG-mahd* The sacred scriptures of ECKANKAR. The scriptures are comprised of about twelve volumes in the spiritual worlds. The first two were transcribed from the inner PLANES by PAUL TWITCHELL, modern-day founder of ECKANKAR.

SOUL. The True Self. The inner, most sacred part of each person. Soul exists before birth and lives on after the death of the physical body. As a spark of God, Soul can see, know, and perceive all things. It is the creative center of Its own world.

SOUL TRAVEL. The expansion of consciousness. The ability of SOUL to transcend the physical body and travel into the spiritual worlds of God. Soul Travel is taught only by the LIVING ECK

MASTER. It helps people unfold spiritually and can provide proof of the existence of God and life after death.

SOUND AND LIGHT OF ECK. The Holy Spirit. The two aspects through which God appears in the lower worlds. People can experience them by looking and listening within themselves and through SOUL TRAVEL.

SPIRITUAL EXERCISES OF ECK. The daily practice of certain techniques to get us in touch with the Light and Sound of God.

SRI. *SREE* A title of spiritual respect, similar to reverend or pastor, used for those who have attained the Kingdom of God. In ECKANKAR, it is reserved for the MAHANTA, the LIVING ECK MASTER.

SUGMAD. *SOOG-mahd* A sacred name for God. Sugmad is neither masculine nor feminine; It is the source of all life.

TEMPLE(S) OF GOLDEN WISDOM. These Golden Wisdom Temples are spiritual temples which exist on the various PLANES—from the Physical to the Anami Lok; CHELAS of ECKANKAR are taken to the temples in the SOUL body to be educated in the divine knowledge; the different sections of the SHARIYAT-KI-SUGMAD, the sacred teachings of ECK, are kept at these temples.

TWITCHELL, PAUL. An American ECK MASTER who brought the modern teachings of ECKANKAR to the world through his writings and lectures. His spiritual name is Peddar Zaskq.

VAIRAG. *vie-RAHG* Detachment.

WAH Z. *WAH zee* The spiritual name of SRI HAROLD KLEMP. It means the Secret Doctrine. It is his name in the spiritual worlds.

For more explanations of ECKANKAR terms, see *A Cosmic Sea of Words: The ECKANKAR Lexicon* by Harold Klemp.

Discover spiritual truth through past lives, dreams, and Soul Travel
Free Eckankar book reveals how

A seeker from New York wrote, "I received your packet and read your book, which was extremely helpful to me. Thank you."

Hundreds of thousands of people around the globe have read *ECKANKAR—Ancient Wisdom for Today* in more than seven languages. And so many have benefited spiritually.

A Florida newspaper praised this book: "Fascinating and well worth reading as you bring deeper spiritual insight into your life."

You'll see how **past lives** affect every aspect of your life. The way you handle relationships. Make choices. Face challenges.

You'll learn through your own experience that **dreams** are real. They help you make better decisions. Lose the fear of dying—and living—by understanding them.

Using a special technique, you'll find how **Soul Travel** is a natural method for intuitively seeing the big picture and discover spiritual truth for yourself. Begin the adventure of a lifetime *today*.

To get your free copy of *ECKANKAR—Ancient Wisdom for Today* (a $4.95 value), go to Eckankar's Web site at

www.eckankar.org
or call ☎ 1-800-LOVE GOD
(1-800-568-3463)
toll-free, 24 hours a day. Ask for book #BK45.

Or you can write to: ECKANKAR, Dept. BK45, PO Box 2000, Chanhassen, MN 55317-2000 USA.

For Further Reading and Study

Past Lives, Dreams, and Soul Travel
Harold Klemp

What if you could recall past-life lessons for your benefit today? What if you could learn the secret knowledge of dreams to gain the wisdom of the heart? Or Soul Travel, to master the shift in consciousness needed to find peace and contentment? To ride the waves of God's love and mercy? Let Harold Klemp, leading authority in all three fields, show you how.

How to Survive Spiritually in Our Times,
Mahanta Transcripts, Book 16
Harold Klemp

A master storyteller, Harold Klemp weaves stories, tips, and techniques into the golden fabric of his talks. They highlight the deeper truths within you, so you can apply them in your life *now*. He speaks right to Soul. It is that divine, eternal spark that you are. The survivor. Yet survival is only the starting point in your spiritual life. Harold Klemp also shows you how to gain in spiritual wealth. This book's a treasure.

Those Wonderful ECK Masters
Harold Klemp

Could you be one of the countless people who have been touched by a meeting with an ECK Master? These real-life stories and spiritual exercises can awaken you to the presence and help of these spiritual guides. Since the beginning of time they have offered guidance, protection, and divine love to help you fulfill your spiritual destiny.

Autobiography of a Modern Prophet
Harold Klemp

Master your true destiny. Learn how this man's journey to God illuminates the way for you too. Dare to explore the outer limits of the last great frontier, your spiritual worlds! The more you explore them, the sooner you come to discovering your true nature as an infinite, eternal spark of God. This book helps you get there! A good read.

Available from your local bookstores, online bookstores, and www.eckankar.org. Or call (952) 380-2222, or write ECKANKAR, Dept. BK45, PO Box 2000, Chanhassen, MN 55317-2000 USA.

There May Be an Eckankar Study Group near You

Eckankar offers a variety of local and international activities for the spiritual seeker. With hundreds of study groups worldwide, Eckankar is near you! Many areas have Eckankar centers where you can browse through the books in a quiet, unpressured environment, talk with others who share an interest in this ancient teaching, and attend beginning discussion classes on how to gain the attributes of Soul: wisdom, power, love, and freedom.

Around the world, Eckankar study groups offer special one-day or weekend seminars on the basic teachings of Eckankar. For membership information, visit the Eckankar Web site (www.eckankar.org). For the location of the Eckankar center or study group nearest you, click on "Eckankar in Your Area" for a listing of those areas with Web sites. You're also welcome to check your phone book under **ECKANKAR**; call **(952) 380-2222, Ext. BK45;** or write **ECKANKAR, Att: Information, BK45, PO Box 2000, Chanhassen, MN 55317-2000 USA.**

☐ Please send me information on the nearest Eckankar center or study group in my area.

☐ Please send me more information about membership in Eckankar, which includes a twelve-month spiritual study.

Please type or print clearly

Name _____
       first (given)   last (family)

Street _____ Apt. # _____

City _____ State/Prov. _____

Zip/Postal Code _____ Country _____

About Harold Klemp

Harold Klemp was born in Wisconsin and grew up on a small farm. He attended a two-room country schoolhouse before going to high school at a religious boarding school in Milwaukee, Wisconsin.

After preministerial college in Milwaukee and Fort Wayne, Indiana, he enlisted in the U.S. Air Force. There he trained as a language specialist at Indiana University and a radio intercept operator at Goodfellow AFB, Texas. Then followed a two-year stint in Japan where he first encountered Eckankar.

In October 1981, he became the spiritual leader of Eckankar, Religion of the Light and Sound of God. His full title is Sri Harold Klemp, the Mahanta, the Living ECK Master. As the Living ECK Master, Harold Klemp is responsible for the continued evolution of the Eckankar teachings.

His mission is to help people find their way back to God in this life. Harold Klemp travels to ECK seminars in North America, Europe, and the South Pacific. He has also visited Africa and many countries throughout the world, meeting with spiritual seekers and giving inspirational talks. There are many videocassettes and audiocassettes of his public talks available.

In his talks and writings, Harold Klemp's sense of humor and practical approach to spirituality have helped many people around the world find truth in their lives and greater inner freedom, wisdom, and love.

International Who's Who of Intellectuals
Ninth Edition

Reprinted with permission of Melrose Press Ltd., Cambridge, England, excerpted from *International Who's Who of Intellectuals, Ninth Edition,* Copyright 1992 by Melrose Press Ltd.